Country
CHIC

COUNTRY LIVING

Country
CHIC

Country Style for Modern Living

Liz Bauwens &
Alexandra Campbell

Photography by Simon Brown

Hearst Books

New York

First Edition

10 9 8 7 6 5 4 3 2 1

Library of Congress Cataloging-in-Publication Data

Country chic : country style for modern living
      p. cm.
   ISBN 1-58816-016-5
      1. Decoration and ornament, Rustic. 2. Interior decoration.

   NK1986.R8 C665 2001
   747–dc21   00-058079

Book design by David Fordham
Edited by Mary Lambert

Printed in USA

www.countryliving.com

CONTENTS

INTRODUCTION

EVERYONE HAS A DREAM of the perfect country house: a beautiful, warm, and welcoming place with a sense of comfort and style that comes naturally. The word "country" today evokes a timeless simplicity. A place where classic form is married to modern-day living; where color and pattern are used informally – and sometimes to dramatic effect; and where personal style is not only encouraged, but celebrated.

In a world where brands have become global, country style also knows no boundaries. It is as suitable for a lakeside cabin as it is for a New York City townhouse. It lives as comfortably on the coast as it does in the Great Plains. And, whether you have a gardener's cottage, a New England cape, a California bungalow, or a midwestern ranch, the country look is as appropriate as it is accessible – even on a limited budget.

In this book we take a look at today's modern country style. The houses and apartments featured on the following pages are all real homes. Their decorative schemes have evolved naturally rather than having been designed. And each shows a different, but successful interpretation of today's country look – one that belies location or architectural character.

It is, however, the focus on personal style that gives country its overall appeal. The mixing and matching of different colors, materials, and furnishings; the combination of fine antiques with inexpensive "finds"; and the blending of old with new. Like the clothes that we wear, personal style plays an important role in the way we decorate our homes. So much so, that we decided to borrow a word long associated with fashion to describe the new direction of country today… we call it "Country Chic."

Nancy Soriano
Editor-in-Chief
Country Living

Country
KITCHENS

Warmth and welcome are the words that define a country kitchen, but the casual mix of old and new, along with a sense of light and space, can be achieved in country, town, or city homes. Choose your color schemes from the garden outside — whether it's a window box or a vista of rolling fields — and use tactile natural wood and earthy ceramics.

SHAKER

RIGHT: The red cotton checked curtains add some visual warmth to the room; without them, a cool scheme of green, blue, and white would be too austere.

LEFT: The kitchen table is made from maple, and copied from one in Hancock Shaker Village, Massachusetts. The kitchen counters are also maple to match, because mixing light and dark woods in the same room destroys visual continuity.

THE COUNTRY KITCHEN STANDS for a warm welcome and good food – a place where friends and family can relax and enjoy themselves. Visually, those elements translate into simple, timeless designs, natural woods, an inviting atmosphere of sunlight pouring through the window and cheerful, innocent patterns. There is nothing pretentious about the country kitchen, and yet it's too easy to lose the concept in a jumble of clutter. That is why Shaker style, with its formula of "beauty based on utility," has become a classic. This city basement was the prototype design for Shaker Kitchens, and was created by Liz Shirley of the Shaker Shop in London.

She first had to overcome a problem that many homes have – a room with poor natural light. She removed a dividing wall between it and another room to increase the sense of light and space, and then she set to work on the kitchen's design and color scheme.

LEFT: The sink and things related to wet activities, such as dishwashers or washing machines, are in a small utility area just off the main kitchen to free up living space. The maple "heart" breadboards come from The Shaker Shop.

BELOW: Decorative detail was always plain and simple on all Shaker items. But there is a beauty in its simplicity; here the heart pattern used on the breadboards repeats on the napkins (BOTTOM).

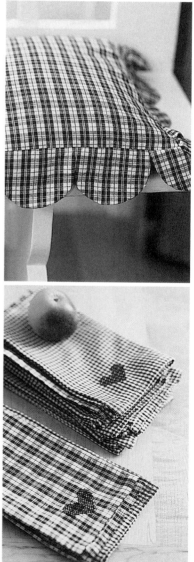

WOODS, PAINTED OR NATURAL?

MOST PEOPLE HAVE ONE or two things that travel with them from house to house.
For Liz Shirley, this was an old Victorian pine dresser and an Aga kitchen range. The
kitchen was then "built around" these two starting points. The maple kitchen table
was copied from one in Hancock Shaker Village, Massachusetts, and the rest of the
wood in the kitchen is also maple to maintain continuity. The cupboard, which was
in a different wood, was painted in the same green as the built-in cabinets – a
delicate duck egg green from Martha Stewart's Arucana colors.

There are an enormous number of possessions to be stored in kitchens today, and,
since this kitchen is also a dining room, Liz Shirley wanted to ensure that everything
could be put away unobtrusively. She based her storage ideas on the walls of kitchen
cabinets and doors that she had seen at Pleasant Hill Shaker Village, Kentucky.
Here, an entire wall of drawers and cupboards housed the summer/winter clothes of
the Shaker community, with each drawer carved to the exact size of the clothes to be
stored, and filled with newly laundered clothes. By adapting the same practice of
deciding exactly what she wanted to store under the stairs and measuring the
cupboards and drawers to fit, she has managed to instal a giant refrigerator, a large
drawer for pots and pans, a cutlery and table linens' drawer, and a cupboard for vases
and candle holders. Using this method, she has kept most of the kitchen
paraphernalia stored in one place. There are two more narrow cupboards for
everything else, on either side of the Aga, each designed to look like another table
pushed into the recess, although they are, in reality, fitted pieces of furniture.

LEFT: The Shaker kitchen is timeless and clean-lined enough to mix with almost any kind of china or cookware, but here the country feel is maintained with an old-fashioned kettle (TOP) rough earthenware bowls (CENTER) and classic steel colander (BOTTOM). There is no pattern anywhere, just neutral or natural colors, and this helps pull the disparate elements together.

RIGHT: The Aga kitchen range with a Shaker peg rail overhead. The peg rail was a key element in Shaker design, with wall space used for storage whenever possible. Here the rail is mainly decorative, but is also used for kitchen implements. The heart symbol was used as a Shaker signature to denote piety; "hands to work and hearts to God" was the credo of the community.

RIGHT: The area under the
stairs has been maximized
as storage space by
copying the Shaker storage
principles of making
cupboards and drawers to
fit each item exactly.

LEFT: A narrow fitted
closet houses the boiler.
The "flyscreen" mesh
allows air to escape.

LEFT: A Victorian pine
cupboard is painted duck-
egg green in order to
avoid showing too many
different types of woods.

It is a key element in the Shaker look that furniture is kept plain, with simple, round knobs and no beading or paneling. Although the Shakers did have decorative features, such as the heart or the Tree of Life, these were used sparingly, as a kind of signature at the end of a piece of work rather than as a repeated pattern.

It is ironic that the Shakers actually scorned beauty. As Shaker Elder Frederick Evans of the Mount Lebanon community said: "The beautiful... is absurd and abnormal. The divine man has no right to waste money upon what you call beauty in his house... while there are people living in misery." Yet it was this very determination to strip away unnecessary frills and ornamentation, and the belief that good design was based on function, that led to the making of beautiful, pared-down designs that have become forerunners of modern furniture. The essence is extreme simplicity – beds were not four-posters and did not have tall bedposts, chairs used the minimum of wood that would make them functional, tables were made simply of legs and a top, and the only decoration was either a coat of paint or a wash that allowed the natural wood grain to show through. Otherwise, wood was left natural. In this respect, 200-year-old Shaker designs are as contemporary as anything made today. Shaker manufacturing techniques were also surprisingly modern. Baskets, for example, were made with efficient "factory-line" methods, albeit with people taking the place of machines.

ABOVE: The key to these arrangements is not to over style them, and to use just one or two kinds of flowers rather than a wide variety. Add greenery from your garden. Miniatures of Shaker-styled furniture (CENTER) can also make a charming mantelpiece display, along with humble spring flowers.

BOXES AND BASKETS

THE SHAKERS WERE FAMOUS for having a place for everything and keeping everything in its place, and they lived by the principle that everything you did, you should do as well as you could to honor God. Shaker communities came to North America mainly from northern Europe, and emigrated from England, Sweden, and other countries. They brought together their native design traditions, then perfected and simplified them. The famous oval Shaker boxes originated in Sweden, but it was the Shaker communities who added swallow-tailed joins and used copper tacks to prevent rusting.

The credo of the Shaker communities was "beauty rests on utility" and, although the communities lasted less than 200 years in relatively small clusters in the northeast, they have had a great impact on our lives through several inventions and adaptations. The flat broom that is used around the world today, the apple corer and the buzz saw were all Shaker inventions.

These designs are popular today, and can be mixed with other styles. Plan a Shaker room, or just a Shaker peg rail. Where there are no Shaker equivalents – the style of flower arrangements, for example – bring in the principles by using natural materials that have been elegantly but simply arranged, carved, or turned. The flowers, boxes, and baskets shown here all copy Shaker principles. Unpretentious spring flowers such as hyacinths, for example, are displayed in a plain basket with garden greenery. This simple display shows the Shaker ability to honor beauty from nature without making it over-elaborate.

RIGHT: Authentic copies of a Shaker table and chairs.

BELOW: Shaker boxes were adapted and improved by the Shaker communities from an old Swedish design, and now the adaptation continues to make the boxes work for 21ˢᵗ-century living. Shaker brooms (BOTTOM) re-shaped household brooms all over the world.

NEW TRADITIONAL

LEFT: French country china (from Elizabeth Bauer in Bath, England,) mixes eclectically with a check tablecloth and other hearty peasant pottery. The Hawaiian dancer in the background supplies a quirky note.

RIGHT and ABOVE: Take your inspiration from the view outside your window. A color scheme of lilac and soft blue was inspired by a lilac tree interwoven with clematis in the garden.

THE RE-USE, RE-CONDITIONING, AND re-cycling of traditional materials to create a contemporary feel is at the heart of both this kitchen and From Somewhere, the knitwear design business of its owner Sasha de Stroumillo. With her partner Orsola de Castro, she re-works discarded knitwear, cutting up and re-stitching, patching or embroidering it into quirky, flattering designs, mixing the new and the old to create something unique. Here, a mass-market kitchen has been transformed into something that feels handmade and authentic by clever repainting and decorating techniques.

Faced with an outdated kitchen, many people would have started again, but this is not Sasha's philosophy. Theoretically a "traditional" country kitchen, Sasha lightened and updated the look of the harsh "orangey" pine cabinet fronts by removing their heavy relief panels and knobs, painting them creamy white and inserting holes instead of handles.

LEFT: Mixing classic rustic patterns, such as barleytwist china and check napkins (TOP) always works well. Cow parsley and anemones (CENTER) echo the paint colors in the room. Sasha de Stroumillo collects and mixes bubble glass (BELOW) in different colors. A mixture of styles and colors works well in glass for an informal, friendly look.

RIGHT: The kitchen table is the central work zone of the room, offering the main space for preparing and eating food, as well as being where the From Somewhere knitwear design business was started. The curtains are made from antique bedspreads.

LEFT: Recycling is at the heart of this kitchen. By replacing the units' handles with holes, removing heavy relief panels, and painting them white, a standard "country" kitchen is given a face-lift which makes it look custom-made. Adding a real wood work surface also makes the rest of the kitchen look much more authentic.

COLORS FROM THE GARDEN

THE KITCHEN'S COLOR SCHEME is a contemporary take on traditional colors too, borrowed from the garden, where a lilac tree blooms, entwined with the gray-green leaves and pinky-white flowers of a clematis. This combination of a soft, back-to-nature green, lilac, and creamy white is the basis for the room, with the kitchen units painted white to make them lighter. The walls have been painted lilac and the tiles and inside of the cupboards green, which looks particularly attractive against white china and clear glass. Changing a few key elements of the room – for example, adding a quality maple work surface, instead of a cheap standard one, and changing the hob top for a stylish stainless steel one – make the most impact on the room, but at a very reasonable cost. The floor was made from inexpensive floorboards that were painted white – a practical way to make the room seem larger and lighter.

ABOVE: Plain china and clear glass storage jars (ABOVE LEFT) offer visual continuity, and prevent clutter from looking like chaos. Small details count – such as painting the inside of the cupboards green to match the tiles. When choosing faucet fittings (TOP), the simplest, cleanest lines will bridge the gap between classic and contemporary.

WELCOMING CLUTTER

NO COUNTRY KITCHEN, however, is without some clutter. Mixed collections of china, mementoes, invitations, reminders of family life, flowers, candle holders, and diverse *objets trouvés* pile up in a friendly and welcoming way. While the owners have the option to keep everything out of sight, the basis of their kitchen is to have it all on display, which is where the trusty traditional cabinet comes in. A cabinet, either pine or painted, fitted or free-standing, is probably the key element that classifies a kitchen as "country" – it is the ingredient that will not be found in a steel urban kitchen. Many people recall the cabinet from their country childhoods, and this one still has traces of its original Victorian painted surface. Similar designs are still widely available today, and can be painted in historic colors or distressed finishes to achieve the effect. Piled high with well-loved collections, it stands as a piece of tradition among contemporary surroundings.

This is a kitchen where pattern and color can sit comfortably together. The curtains are two old floral bedspreads, which turned out to be too long for the windows. However, the strip of fabric that had to be cut off came in useful to make curtain ties. The flowers echo the lilac walls in their blooms, and the yellow of the curtains is repeated in the yellow blind.

In the summer, the big glass doors open up and the kitchen appears to be part of the garden, with soft natural colors inside melding with the real hues of nature outside. You could be in a rural paradise, but, in fact, a busy main street is situated only minutes away.

RIGHT: This antique pine cabinet still has traces of its original Victorian paint. Leaving it intact, rather than renovating it to make it look new, gives the room the feeling that it has always stood there. Don't make old furniture look too restored; the patina of age lends character to a room.

SIMPLICITY

Reinterpret how traditional materials and patterns are used to create a sense of freedom and an uncluttered lifestyle. Simplicity has always been at the heart of country style and features local materials, patterns, and craftsmanship rather than elaborate furnishings.

FLORALS

LEFT: Juxtapose a modern painting with a piece of traditional craftwork or an antique. The yellow in this abstract painting by Terry Frost is echoed in a few other yellow touches in the room, and also in this flower (RIGHT).

FLORALS ARE THE QUINTESSENTIAL country design and can be found on tapestry, needlework, printed cottons and linens, on china, and in paintings. Many of the colors and patterns we all recognize as design classics are inspired by gardens and fields. When combined with simple shapes and modern elements, old favorites gain a new dimension – the basic key is to use florals discreetly, or as decorative accents, in simple contemporary rooms to create a fresh, yet sophisticated, feel.

Florals are wonderfully fresh, vivid and colorful, and work equally well in both contemporary and traditional schemes. And, of course, flowers are at the very heart of the countryside. There is nothing like a bunch of humble *ranunculus* casually placed in a jelly jar, an innocent pot of primroses, or a bouquet of fully blown garden roses to evoke the feeling that there is a luscious green garden, rolling woods and hedgerows situated just outside the door, rather than a busy city street.

CONTEMPORARY FLORALS

THIS ROOM IS A FORMAL town-house drawing room, which many people might be tempted to decorate with "important" furniture and expensive window treatments. However, the owners wanted to emphasize the feelings of light and space, and they both have contemporary tastes. Gardening, in particular, is one of their passions, so the idea of introducing a floral theme is very appropriate and draws the garden from the outdoors into the room.

The starting point for the room was an understated treatment based on white walls and modern furniture from department stores in plain colors and natural fabrics. Such simplicity and discipline balance the wildness of the flowers: the chairs and sofa have a discreet scattering of floral cushions to add an accent, the white background to the fabric echoing the white of the walls. There is a creamy white jug of informal mixed flowers and a few neatly stitched flower-covered lavender bags on the mantelpiece, and, when tea is brought, floral plates with a white background make the perfect china. Nothing is overdone – the temptation to add floral china vases, floral rugs, or chairs covered in floral fabrics has been avoided to keep the room as fresh and light as possible. The pillows haven't been matched – there are, in fact, several different designs in the room, but they are similar enough – all are rosy with sprigs of flowers on a white background. Even the patterns are discreet and self-effacing; small-sprig florals are traditionally the decoration for cottages.

BELOW: Mix ages and styles: here contemporary department-store furniture looks good with collected pieces in a period house. The mantelpiece (LEFT) seems like stone, but was actually built from MDF (medium density fiberboard) by builders, then painted. The chair (CENTER) features just one floral cushion as a striking accent. Contrast is also important in this light, contemporary style. Here an antique table and clock (RIGHT) sit happily with a modern painting and some expensive Shaker boxes.

THE UNDERSTATED LOOK

WHITE IS A PARTICULARLY adaptable base to start with, but versatility can also be achieved with duck-egg blue, soft misty or minty greens, or neutral shades such as bone, ivory, beige, or string. "Historic" paint shades, or cool, clear contemporary tints would make a good base color for floral rooms, but to keep the look simple, try to avoid featuring too many colors in the room.

The palette of this room is essentially white, green, and yellow, while the odd dash of red in the rose pattern of the floral pillows adds that extra splash of color. You can achieve a similar effect by using the shades in any part of the room – yellow walls with green or white chairs and sofas, or the green on the walls with yellow and white, and so on.

Colors that work well with florals include all the shades that are found in nature: from grass green to deepest moss; buttercup and daffodil yellows; hyacinth and forget-me-not blues; and the entire range of rose pinks, from the softest blush to a deep damson red. Your entire color scheme could develop from the shades in one scrap of favorite floral fabric, or from the flowers in your garden: lilac and green, for example, or blue and green. If you find that it starts to get too busy or the overall look seems too florid or overpowering, just introduce some neutral white or cream to calm the whole scheme down.

ABOVE: Simple shapes and neutral colors keep the look uncluttered: a Shaker sewing box, a creamy pottery jar, and a simple vase with one flower in it (LEFT). Plain white china or clear glass makes an ideal foil for flowers of all kinds. Elaborate vases in a floral scheme would make it look too fussy (RIGHT).

ABOVE: A traditional tartan traveling rug, trimmed with velvet and updated by soft hues, blends in with the floral scheme (LEFT). Small sprigs of floral colors always work well together (TOP).

LEFT: Details that count in floral decoration: beaded table mats and a napkin ring delicately made in the shape of a bee (TOP), a pretty blue embroidered bag (CENTER), and a pile of soft luxurious suede notebooks in shades of rose, lilac, and daffodil (BOTTOM).

RIGHT: A delicately stylized floral tablecloth. Different floral fabrics can work well together (FAR RIGHT). Calm Swiss embroidery is making a comeback (BOTTOM LEFT). The greens and pinks of the wallpaper appear again in this vase of flowers (BOTTOM RIGHT).

SIMPLICITY WITH FLORALS

Flowers and floral designs are among the world's best-loved patterns, but such popularity has also, on occasion, been their downfall. It is only a short step from a classic to a cliché, and, as a result, florals go through cycles in and out of fashion. However, this easy, relaxed style of decorating does not follow fashion slavishly – if you have a floral pattern that you love, use it regardless of trends.

Florals lost their reputation when they were married over-fussily to swags and frills, cluttered up with trinkets, and suffocated in pomp and scatter pillows. The key to a contemporary touch with flowers is to let them breathe. Simple, unfussy backgrounds, such as plain cotton or linen upholstered sofas and chairs, white or simply painted walls and understated styling let the charm of floral designs emerge as stars in their own right.

Either traditional or modern patterns look good; just because you have contemporary tastes, there is no need to keep to stylized designs, when a Victorian print could look just as good. Different floral patterns work well together, and you can also add other decorative textures, such as beading, embroidery, mirror mosaic, or soft, pastel shades of suede and silk, and finish it all off with a bunch of artlessly arranged real flowers.

TEXTURES

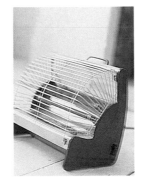

RIGHT: The fragrance of incense stimulates the senses, enhancing the feeling of peace and serenity in the room. A shiny metallic electric fire (ABOVE) is an effective contrast to the natural wool and wood textures in the rest of the room.

LEFT: The walls are painted in a simple and sophisticated gray-tinged mushroom white. The fireplace is not used, but is kept opened up, so that it looks as if you could light a fire when you wanted. The roughness of the bricks and the original floorboards contrast with the sleek modern lines; when you are modernizing, don't change everything.

THE USE OF TEXTURE rather than pattern is one of the ways that country elements can be used in sophisticated urban surroundings to introduce a feeling of serenity and calm. Decorating with texture is about appreciating the true nature of surfaces, rather than covering up or disguising them. This home belongs to stylist and furniture designer, Janie Jackson, who runs a decorative design company called Parma Lilac. The house is based in an elegant part of town, but it is light and airy enough to be a home by the sea.

Minimalism is the key to this look – bare boards and brick, white paint, and a few understated pieces of furniture. The lack of fussy detail means that even a relatively small room can be made to feel spacious, and there is a certain barefoot chic about it that is balm to the soul.

The colors in a textured room are usually neutrals and naturals, ranging from white and bone to the shades of pebbles and animal hide, and dark shades such as charcoal.

DISCIPLINED STYLE

THE ORDERLY AND ALMOST monastic atmosphere of this sunny bedroom is preserved through rigorous discipline. In a crowded world where material possessions are prized and usually a priority, it can be liberating to be ruthless in editing what you wear and what you have around you, because it literally gives you space to think. The philosophy of making your life simpler by buying or using only possessions that you really love or need may not be easy, and Janie Jackson admits to thinking very carefully before she buys anything and also to clearing out when clutter creeps in. Her efforts are worthwhile, for they give her the pleasure of waking up in a peaceful, airy, almost empty bedroom with sunlight streaming through the shutters.

The bed with its streamlined steel legs and base was designed by Janie Jackson, and is lighter and more airy-looking than the usual divan beds with their chunky bases. It sits relatively high; there is space underneath for storing boxes and baskets, or it could be left as a clutter-free space.

Simple white cotton or linen bedding is the only option for such a calm environment, and a textured wool blanket from Wales adds an element of interest to the smooth surfaces of steel and white paint.

The shutters are particularly clever, as they are made of Perspex and designed by Janie Jackson to offer a practical, contemporary alternative to curtains. They allow for privacy, but let in light and are less heavy and domineering than wooden shutters.

No art or ornament is required in a room like this; some pebbles from a beach or smooth black stones are all that are needed to remind you of nature's beauty.

OPPOSITE : The contrast of smooth walls, slightly gleaming painted floorboards and the roughness of the pebbles (ABOVE) and the woolen Welsh blanket make texture, rather than color, the key to achieving a look like this. Note the Perspex shutters (INSET) which filter light while offering privacy.

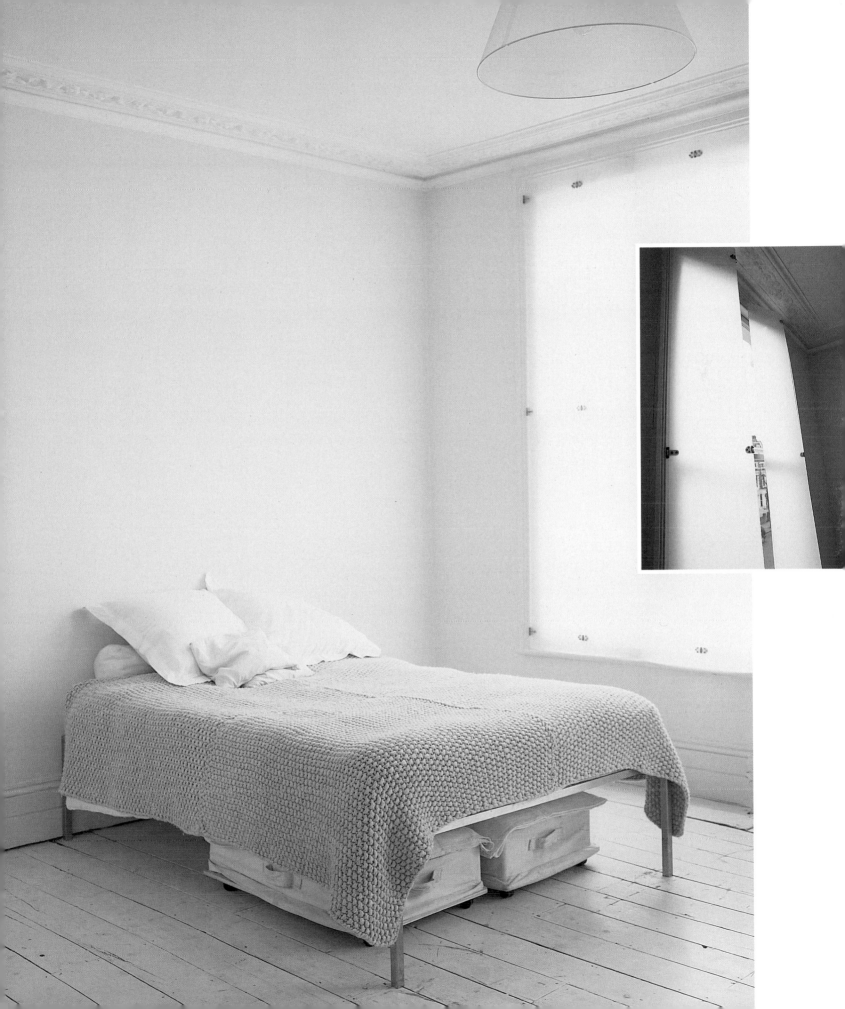

ABOVE AND LEFT: Texture is at its most satisfying in traditional materials: wool, wood, steel, and glass, like those contained in this vase and bedspread. They have a depth that is lacking in plastics. Mix round and smooth textures, and look for natural objects, such as alliums, that have architectural shapes, in order to achieve the feel of a timeless but contemporary summer house situated in the woods.

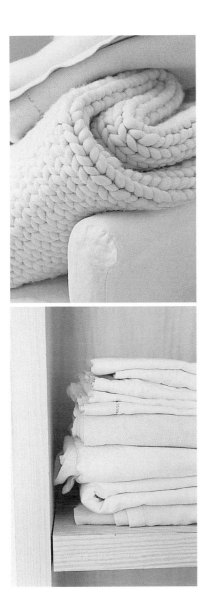

ABOVE: Paint a naturally dark room yellow to maximize a feeling of light (ABOVE RIGHT). Open shelving looks more spacious than covered, and these linens become part of the overall decoration of the room. This is a stylish new idea for storing bedding and towels.

STORAGE AND DECORATION

THIS BEDROOM AND DRESSING ROOM were originally two rooms, but Janie Jackson knocked down the wall between them to open up the space. The front of the house, where the bedroom is, was light and painted white, but the dressing room faced north, so she painted it yellow for warmth. The theme of transparency and freedom from clutter is maintained by open shelves and a plain hanging rail in place of closets. Building shelves on either side of the windows preserved floorspace.

The floors were painted off-white also to maximize the light, and their slightly shiny surfaces reflect the sun too. With just one table and mirror to complete the set-up, the whole room is a pared-down, feminine dressing room. No decoration is needed, because the clothes with their textures of cotton, silk, and wool, are on full view. Their soft colors range from calm neutrals to pastels.

LEFT: Venetian mirrors – where a mirror frame surrounds a central mirror – were fashionable in the 18th and 19th centuries. In a plain, simple room, one outrageous or elaborate item adds impact and character. The lightness achieved by having mirror surrounded by mirror offers a contrast of texture which does not overwhelm. Sitting on a neat table, it also makes an ideal dresser (BELOW).

RIGHT: The carefully planned shelves and open hanging rail were designed by Janie Jackson. This look requires discipline but saves time hunting for clothes in the morning.

TEXTURE IN THE BATHROOM

DECORATING WITH TEXTURE CAN also be done by taking one texture and working with its variations. Here the glassy nature of water reflects the shiny mix of textures for a bathing area. Steel, tin, china, glass, and painted wood harmonize rather than contrast with one another. There is nothing unnecessary in the room: semi-circular stools, also designed by Janie Jackson, are calm and simple, a single faucet combines hot and cold water, and the plumbing of the square china sink is left exposed. Frosted glass is used at the windows, so no curtains are needed, allowing the elegant lines of the sash window to be enjoyed.

Bathrooms in old country houses are often thought of as bleak, chilly outposts – while the ones in towns and cities tend to be associated with luxury and pampering. Yet in today's well-heated homes, a bare, simple bathroom can be like a breath of fresh, country air. It is a modern indulgence to be restrained and plain.

PRACTICAL CONSIDERATIONS

THERE ARE PRACTICAL ASPECTS to simplicity – notably the plumbing. Here the drain of the sink is on full view, but the plumbing behind the single faucet has been concealed. and the pipes have been encased in brickwork and covered with plaster – but it's worth checking with your local plumber and finding out whether the faucet washers will get furred up quickly. You don't want to re-decorate every time you change a washer.

BELOW: As well as contrasting textures, you can also unify them: here, steel, china, and glass echo the shiny surface of water. Use dual-purpose furniture to keep the look simple: semi-circular stools are used to hold towels and bathroom accessories, while a painted table holds a large mirror.

RIGHT: Simplicity means honesty: that is why the metallic waste pipe has been left on view in this minimalist bathroom.

Decorating with
COLOR and PATTERN

PATTERNS, COLOR, AND CLASSIC PATTERNS LIKE FLORALS AND CHECKS USED IN FRESH, CONTEMPORARY WAYS ARE THE SUBSTANCE OF THIS STYLE. YOU CAN ALSO EMULATE A STUNNING, ECLECTIC ATMOSPHERE THAT BORROWS FROM OLD-FASHIONED TRADITIONS AND GIVES THEM A MODERN TWIST.

FADED PATTERNS

A CLASSIC COUNTRY LOOK that nonetheless remains fresh is a relaxed mix of color and pattern, often faded with wear and eclectic in the way it's put together. This is a most welcoming and natural style of decorating, which evolves over the years, and is never quite "finished." It is an organic way of living, which looks pretty but is also primarily practical, and this house, home of the stylist Lucinda Chambers, exemplifies this kind of country style.

Floral patterns, such as chintzes, damasks, and toiles, along with classic stripes, checks and textured plains, plus collections – anything from plates to purses – are at the heart of this unusual, but comfortable look. Everything looks used, because they are used, although many stores now stock fabrics that are made to look "faded" or tea-stained with age in order to re-create a sense of timelessness.

ABOVE: The key to the faded style is that nothing matches: wicker and wooden chairs sit together (LEFT), different classic patterns of Cornish blue-and-white and Denby pottery are combined with more delicate rose-tinted plates (CENTER), and the plates themselves are all bought at random in twos and threes, or singly, from flea markets and second-hand shops (RIGHT).

A THEME OF ROSES

HERE THE KITCHEN IS a glorious home for Lucinda's collection of china, and fabric with roses on it. Old roses and new ones, bright and faded roses, roses from the East and from the West, rosy fabrics, plates, cups, and rosy hues and tints of every kind mingle together in a glorious symphony. Nothing is contrived or arranged, so family and guests feel free to linger and lounge, without worrying about disarranging a carefully thought-out scheme. It's a real home, not a photographic image which will be spoiled when someone throws a school bag or a pile of shopping on the table. It is a home with a heart and soul, not a reflection of fashion.

Although this style seems to have no limits, collections do offer a unifying theme for those who don't know how to achieve a rambling look. Here it is roses, but other themes could be florals in general, shades and patterns in blues, small patterns, checks and stripes, or even a scheme inspired by the colors and patterns of a teapot collection or Thirties' china. The added bonus of these collectibles is that china, glass, fabrics, and furniture don't have to be expensive; many of these plates were found in second-hand stores, and, if one breaks, Lucinda easily replaces it.

A key element of this style is that nothing matches. The dining room chairs are plain wooden kitchen chairs, but in different styles. The detail on the built-in kitchen units varies on either side of the room. On one side, tongue-and-groove boarding is set into a frame, with small inset silver handles. On the other, the detailing is plainer, with old-fashioned steel drawer handles. Both sides are painted white – although they could have easily been painted different colors – and all have steel handles, but that is all that matches.

RIGHT: Mismatched chairs around the kitchen table create a relaxed atmosphere, reflected in an informal bunch of blue and pink flowers in a humble jug. As well as mixing old and new, and different styles, this look juxtaposes the grand and the modest: the fireplace is marble and is usually found in a more formal-looking room. However, here it has an air of faded grandeur.

BELOW: This style is ideal for magpies; anything pretty can be displayed, such as this charming painted wooden egg.

CUSTOM-MADE KITCHENS

THIS KITCHEN WAS DESIGNED by Lucinda Chambers herself. She sketched out what she wanted for the builder to copy. If you can't find what you like in the brochures of kitchen companies, or if you have a house in mind with a distinctive style you'd like to mirror, don't be afraid of having your kitchen units custom built by craftsmen or carpenters. This can be a surprisingly cost-effective option, but plan carefully before having anything built.

This look could be described as organic because it grows with the house, but it must also be practical. The table settles where it is most convenient. An old couch or chair is placed where people like to sit. The closet that contains the vacuum cleaner or broom is kept in the most convenient place, not where a designer has deemed it should go. While the impulse is often to set up the house as soon as you move into it, you might create a more natural feeling if you live somewhere for several months before deciding what you want where. See where the light falls at different times of day, the best seasonal views, and where people like to congregate.

Many of the patterns and styles are classic; if they're not genuinely old, they're patterns that have been in use continuously for a hundred years or more. Amongst such styles are New Jersey stoneware, Mexican maiolica and even the traditional creamware pottery now made by designer Calvin Klein. Either buy the antiques or the modern output to create a house that looks as if it has been lived in for generations.

Opposite: The mantelpiece arrangement is not contrived: like everything else in the house, it has grown organically as pretty treasures are brought home. Valuable items, like silver candle holders, can sit next to flea market finds and smooth stones found on country walks.

BELOW LEFT AND RIGHT: There is a theme of roses in these rooms, and they can be found literally on every surface from china and fabric. Open shelving and a plate rack help to display everything.

BLUE AND WHITE KITCHEN

ABOVE: Blue flowers in white vases mirror the theme of the kitchen.

LEFT: This is another "recycled" kitchen. Here a continuous run of brown Seventies' units were painted white. A good trick to copy includes replacing a few units with a plate rack or basket drawers to break up the run, making it look more modern and less ordered. Add a white fretwork strip at the bottom of the shelves as a pretty decorative effect.

BLUE AND WHITE is a classic color combination, and it's friendly and relaxed, evoking country dairies and the freshness of a simple blue-and-white handstitched quilt. Almost every part of the world has a tradition of using blue and white in kitchens and in cookware, from English striped tea towels and Dutch Delft tiles to the glorious slatey blues of Shaker paint colors or the blue-and-white French enamel kitchenware that is now considered so collectible. The combination of blue and white is fresh, pretty, and contemporary, without being folksy. Most important, the effect looks equally good with any budget, and can be very flexible. This kitchen here, for example, is predominantly white, with the blue appearing in the table linen and china, which means that the emphasis can easily be altered if tastes or fashions change.

The starting point for this kitchen was economy. Replacing a kitchen is often one of the biggest investments made in a house and, when you've just moved in, it's often best

ABOVE: Stripes and checks
are classic patterns for a
blue-and-white theme, and
create a light, fresh
atmosphere.

LEFT: A small bunch of anemones or
ranunculus placed casually in a plain
blue glass vase adds a light, informal
touch to the kitchen. There's no
need to worry about balance or
arrangement – the effect is similar to a
wildflower arrangement with blooms
that have been picked by a child on
a country walk.

to see how you can use the existing kitchen before you spend a lot of money on a new one. Faced with an outdated brown L-shaped kitchen, the owner, Suzanne Sharp of The Rug Company, made it feel instantly lighter and more modern by painting the units white. She believes that painting something white to brighten it up, and then living with it for a while before making more changes, is often the best way to proceed.

CHANGING THE DESIGN

MANY PEOPLE CHANGE the doors on kitchen cabinets to alter the look, but you can create a different feel even more effectively – and cheaply – by remodeling just one or two elements rather than changing the whole lot. Kitchens with continuous runs of units are "modern urban," while those with a mix of furniture and fittings are more likely to be perceived as "country." Simply making your kitchen irregular will make it feel more relaxed. For example, this kitchen had been a continuous L-shape of base and wall cabinets. Suzanne removed two wall cabinets to break the run and open the space, making it feel more organic and relaxed. She also took off some doors – not all – to create some open shelves, and added a wall-hung plate rack. While all the doors on the lower cabinets were retained and painted white, two doors on the upper cabinets were replaced with wooden ones, with the wood laid laterally. The changes were relatively small, but they effectively freed the rigid, outdated design.

Finally, she added a fretwork strip along the bottom of the cabinets. It softens the hard lines of the modern cabinets and is reminiscent of old-fashioned shelves with cotton, embroidered shelf liners.

ABOVE: Food covers (LEFT) were used in old-fashioned kitchens to protect food from being attacked by flies. Now they're making a comeback because so much produce – such as fruit or cheese – tastes better at room temperature. Everyday, inexpensive tumblers (CENTER) add to the informal effect. Collectible blue and white fine china (RIGHT) can also easily be mixed with budget chain-store purchases to great effect.

Mixing closed cabinets with open shelves is an effective way of making a design look more relaxed. The most convenient kitchenware to display on open shelves are those used every day, such as plates and glasses. The one disadvantage of open shelving is that items can get sticky or dusty from the kitchen's atmosphere, but if everything is used frequently, that is not a problem. Open shelves also allow china and glass to become integrated into the decorative scheme.

Keeping to a theme, such as blue, blue-and-white, or white china emphasizes the look, and prevents it from becoming too cluttered and untidy. Odd plates and cups can sit together very attractively, and expensive china can be mixed with cheaper buys to achieve harmony. You can go as far as you like by adding blue-and-white tablecloths and napkins, bowls, jugs, vases, and flowers. Blue and white fabrics can be found in any style, from a traditional Fifties' design like this tablecloth by Cath Kidston, to cheerful farmhouse stripes and checks and vibrantly modern designs.

Flooring is often considered a major decorating challenge in kitchens, because of spilt food and heavy traffic. Many people choose dark colors in the belief that the floor will need less cleaning. However, light floors keep the decorative emphasis on the furnishings and decorations, and also make limited spaces appear bigger. Here the floorboards were simply sanded down and painted white, and they survived several years of family life before they needed re-painting.

ABOVE: The delicate floral pattern of this china and glassware fits well into the blue and white theme.

RIGHT: A bunch of scented spring narcissi blends with the color scheme and adds a wonderful fragrance to the kitchen.

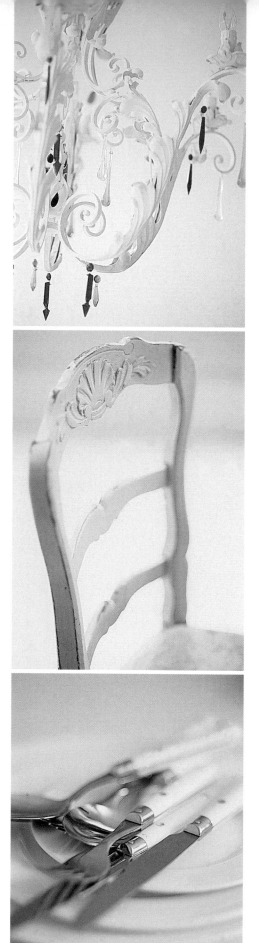

LEFT: Transform heavy items with white paint: an iron chandelier has been painted white, with little glass droplets simply tied on, making it an interesting focal point in the room. Old wooden chairs have been painted a distressed white (CENTER) to give them a friendly freshness reminiscent of Swedish style. China, glass, and cutlery (BOTTOM) have been carefully chosen to maintain the blue-and-white theme.

RIGHT: One single over-sized item in a small room can make it seem bigger and grander than it really is. Here the chandelier fulfils that function well. A comfortable armchair (INSET) in a floral fabric helps to bring a note of comfort to the room.

Elegant dining

THIS GLORIOUSLY LIGHT and refined dining area is adjacent to the blue and white kitchen, and follows its decorative theme in a way that is both understated and grand. The room itself is square with floor-to-ceiling windows. It is not particularly large, but it has a high ceiling. One of the tricks used by interior decorators to make a small area seem larger than it is, is to have one extra-large out-of-scale focal point that makes a stunning single statement. Here the room's main asset, the high ceiling, is used, and the focal statement is a large iron candelabra, again painted white by Suzanne Sharp. It would have been just as dramatic to leave it as its original ironwork, but painting it white makes it lighter and more delicate, and just as outrageous, but not as overbearing. She also added droplets of colored glass in blue and red to emphasize its decorative effect.

A big country kitchen table and some French-looking ladderback chairs, also painted white, along with an old armchair in a faded floral fabric, complete the effect. With the white painted walls and floor, the room needs no more decoration. Including any paintings or ornaments would distract from the sweeping spaciousness that has been evoked by the Swedish elements.

Swedish style has a great deal of influence on today's contemporary interiors, because it is light and modern, yet very decorative. To encapsulate the look, keep windows bare or use simple transparent muslin drapes (light is important in a northern country,) have white, gray, or pastel walls, use candles (on long, dark Swedish nights, they increase the sense of light,) and use wooden furniture, as Sweden is covered in pine forests.

SEASIDE HUES

ABOVE: Displaying beach mementoes such as this starfish, or framing simple objects (RIGHT), is an effective way of displaying collections.

LEFT: Seaside fabrics, such as checks and florals, work well together when the scale of the patterns is similar. The furniture included here shows how different styles can look good together when they are uniformly painted white.

THE SEA AND THE NEARBY COUNTRYSIDE hold evocative memories for most people of long, hot summer holidays. The seaside is a perfect inspiration for decorating, particularly for children's rooms and bathrooms. These children's rooms, designed by Suzanne and Christopher Sharp, have all the naïve charm of a holiday, ranging from the traditional bucket-and-spade summer holiday to the carnival atmosphere and palm-fringed exotica of the tropics.

When taking such a theme as inspiration for decorating, always look at color elements first. The ingredients of the coast are the colors of sea and sand – blue and cream – along with reds and candy pinks, that look so bright under an open sky. All these colors are punctuated with plenty of white.

Then identify typical patterns: seaside fabrics are bright and honest, such as checks and stripes, and the proximity of sun and wind means that many things can look just that little bit worn and faded.

LEFT: Originally from India, these elaborate beds were found in a second-hand store. They were dark teak, but have taken on a completely different look when painted white. Pillows (CENTER) can be trimmed with ribbon and a curtain (BOTTOM) made to look more modern by adding a contrasting hem. The ribbon above and the row of bobbles helps to disguise the fact that they were later additions.

RIGHT: Always try several shades of paint in large panels on several walls before deciding on exactly the right tone of color for a room. A room's natural light changes the way the color appears. This shade of blue looks calm and neutral, evoking the essence of the sea in the northern light of this bedroom, but appears to be almost a turquoise shade in a south-facing room.

HOW TO CHOOSE COLOR

PEOPLE RESPOND INSTINCTIVELY TO COLOR, so pay attention to your own instincts. Start with the colors you love, rather than feel constrained by the colors in vogue. Fashionable colors are more likely to date. Be fearless and try colors that delight you – the key to success is to experiment and be prepared to change something if it doesn't work out. Once you've decided on your favourite color, think in terms of color families, such as pastels, antique colors, brights, neutrals, mid-tones or deep tones. Take your starting color – for example, a soft blue – and look for other shades in a similar family to build your palette. An equally muted green and a faded red would go well with the blue.

Contrast adds life to a scheme, but use it in small doses. Too much makes a room seem busy. Here a black-and-white chair adds a dramatic touch to a colorful room, but a room decorated entirely in black and white would have been excessive. Large areas of contrast often don't work, such as green sofas against a red wall. Try red sofas against a red wall with green cushions.

Another important consideration when choosing color is the natural light in each room. Here, two rooms face north, while the third faces south, and can take bright colors well. The north-facing rooms are the hardest to choose colors for, because bright colors can seem too strong, and paler shades too dull. Blues can be particularly changeable: the blue bedroom, for example, is painted a shade that is delicately neutral in a north-facing room, but almost turquoise in a south-facing room. Paint sample panels on the walls, as Suzanne Sharp did, and take weeks before making your final decision. Choosing a paint from swatches on card simply does not give a true impression of what it will look like on the wall.

ABOVE: A great child's room is a mix of the practical and funky: here a simple, white table from a home store chain makes a useful desk (RIGHT). Quirky objects such as this zebra stool (CENTER) look good in this brightly colored room. To achieve a relaxed, yet coherent effect with pattern, make sure that the colors used are similar as shown here with this attractive jumble of bedlinen (LEFT).

OPPOSITE: The holiday theme is picked up in this room's carnival colors. As it is south-facing, it can take stronger colors, such as this vivid pink. A good trick is to paint half the wall white, as seen here, to make the color look fresher and less dominating. Colors of a similar brightness look good together.

ABOVE: A roman blind offers privacy but keeps the room light and airy.

ABOVE RIGHT: If you have a landing with several rooms leading off it, you can use it to set a theme. Here, tongue and groove boarding up to chest height, and a shelf for memorabilia, show the seaside theme more distinctively than the rooms that lead off it.

FINDING INSPIRATION

Deciding on a theme and making it work in a room means experimenting with what works and what doesn't, but it's worth risking a few mistakes to have a home that you really enjoy rather than one which feels "safe" and ordinary. You can take inspiration from your garden; from a bunch of flowers seen in a florist's window; from the combination of shells and sand on the beach, seawater, and a blue, blue sky; or from the pages of a magazine or book, or a shop window.

Look at the elements: the colors, the objects, and the patterns and begin to set up a swatchboard. This is an interior designer trick: take small pieces of paint or fabric, and pin them together on a board to see how they work. Then switch them around to see how the balance of color and atmosphere changes. Once you have a scheme you like, try it out over as large an area as possible. This doesn't just mean

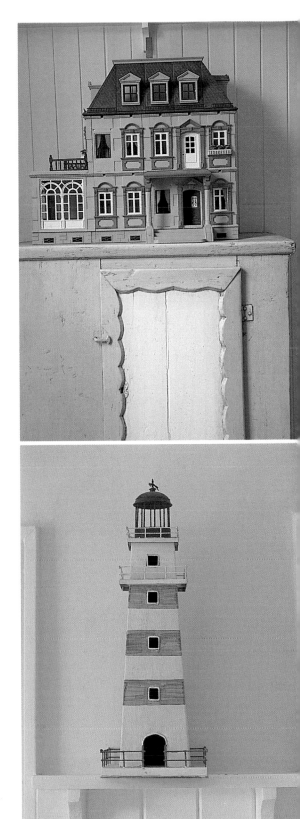

the paint – fabric and flooring are just as important. Many shops will sell large sample swatches of fabric, and then return your money if you return the swatch (this is useful if you're going to buy expensive fabric.) If the fabric is affordable, buy a yard of it and drape it over furniture for a few days to see how it works. If you don't want to paint panels of paint in your room, buy plain lining wallpaper, paint that and pin it up. Reputable rug companies will also lend rugs for a few days so that you see them in situ. Place the chair or sofa you're hoping to re-cover (or a similar one) draped in the fabric swatch, and live with the large-scale re-creation of your swatchboard in one corner until you've decided it's right for the whole room.

THE FINAL TOUCHES

These add the character to a room: the lighthouse, the doll's house, the little beach huts.... If your budget is tight, try searching flea markets for pieces that are a little bit different and can be transformed with fabric, wallpaper, or paint. As their intrinsic value is not great, you can afford to experiment. For these rooms, a kitchen chair and an Indian mirror add character to decor at a very low cost. The chair might be found almost anywhere, but it has been painted white and given a new seat in a vivid fabric. A chair like this gives you a real chance to have fun. It could be painted in bright colors or given an antique look with historic colors and a distressed finish. It could even become ultra-luxurious by adding a small square of a very expensive fabric to the seat. So, if there's a piece of fabric you've fallen in love with but can't afford, this is a great way to add it to your decorative scheme. Not only are these ideas inexpensive, but also they can be done in an afternoon.

The key to successful shopping at second-hand stores is to go in every time you pass one. Piled among the unattractive items of poor quality, there may be one or two that are worth buying, but you need to go regularly to find them. If Suzanne Sharp sees something she likes, she buys it, regardless of whether she really needs it, because she knows that she will never find exactly the same thing again.

ABOVE: Tongue-and-groove boarding and a peg rail create a seaside/country feel. A display cabinet can be used to hold holiday treasures.

BELOW: A wire basket makes a useful container for bathroom knick-knacks or *objet trouvés*.

THE BATHROOM

A BATHROOM CAN BE the ultimate fantasy room. Small enough to make expensive paint or paper affordable, it can be re-decorated quickly if you tire of the theme. It is a room to relax in – a place where you can be whisked away mentally to another world. But is not a room where you linger as long as in kitchens, living rooms, and bedrooms, so there is less chance of getting bored with the decoration.

A nautical or seaside fantasy is one of the most attractive themes for bathrooms, and can be easy to achieve, even with mass-market fittings and in a tiny space. This bathroom was created on a strict budget, with all the fixtures, fittings, and tongue and groove boarding coming from a do-it-yourself chain, and basic pine shelving.

Once you have bought the basics – a white bathroom suite, shelving, towel rails and somewhere to keep bathroom paraphernalia, you can let your imagination fly. Some interior decorators believe that color is the last thing to add. So get the bathroom layout and fittings right, and then choose the room's color.

CHOOSING A COLOR

ALTHOUGH YOU CAN USE WALLPAPER in a bathroom – the steam is less damaging than you might expect and you'll get a good few years of wear out of it – paint is usually a better option. If you've inherited a bathroom that you don't like, try painting it to lift the atmosphere before replacing it altogether. (However, it is difficult to paint tiles well, and it can look cheap.) If you can't afford to re-tile, cover it up with plyboard or tongue-and-groove boarding. If the area is regularly splashed, such as the wall near the shower, it will need re-painting more often, although today's acrylic paints are fairly water-resistant. Here, paint has been used to make inexpensive pine look timeless and chic.

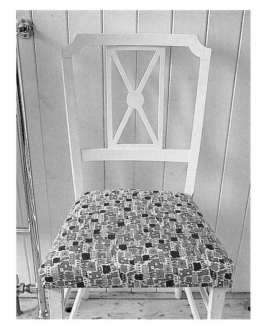

ABOVE: A junk-shop chair can be transformed by using a fun fabric on the seat.

RIGHT: A shelf above tongue-and-groove boarding in the bathroom offers another opportunity to display themed items, as well as being a useful place for shampoo bottles and other bathroom paraphernalia. A display case protects more treasured items.

Natural
ELEMENTS

THE GRAIN OF REAL WOOD IS A STARTING POINT FOR TWO VERY DIFFERENT
DECORATING APPROACHES: THE CALM, CLEAN, PURITANICAL DESIGNS
EVOKED BY TRADITIONAL NEW ENGLAND, AND A MODERN DESIGN THAT
HAPPILY MIXES WOOD WITH MAN-MADE MATERIALS.

NEW ENGLAND

LEFT AND ABOVE: A simple trestle table and Wishbone chairs are the only furniture in the dining end of this double room. The brick surroundings and the wood of the log fire look almost like a work of art against the white walls.

THE SNOWY VASTNESS OF New England – the mountains, and pine trees, the long winters, and the simplicity of the clapboard houses – is evoked here in a contemporary white-and-wood room in a town basement. The clarity of the mountain air, the sense of space, and the grainy, satisfying texture of wood are the inspiration, letting you believe that you are in a mountain hideaway in the woods, rather than in a busy city. When settlers first arrived on the East Coast, they brought the house-building skills and tastes of northern Europe with them, but new architectural and interior styles soon evolved. The tough life and scarcity of raw materials – except for wood – meant that houses were simple and box-like. They were made of clapboard (this term refers to the noise of board hitting board as the house was built) with little detailing, either inside or out. This look has now become synonymous with chic modern style, yet still evokes a simpler time.

LEFT: Complement a simple, understated decor with elegant pottery in neutral and natural colors.

ABOVE: An old wooden trestle against white-painted tongue-and-groove creates a rustic yet airy effect.

RIGHT: Washable loose covers are practical and stylish on white armchairs, and the effect of white on white makes the room seem bigger and lighter.

PRACTICAL STYLE

The white painted bare boards and walls are the starting point for this look and the rest of the room is restrained. It could almost be called stark, except for the warmth and smoothness of the wooden chairs; they are modern designs, known as Wishbone chairs, but were purchased in an antique market. Many pieces of modern furniture have become design classics, and purchasing them second-hand is a good way of acquiring them at a reasonable price. There is an added attraction to them in that wood acquires a friendly patina when it is used and worn; chairs straight from the factory would not have quite the same depth of tone. The dining table is a simple trestle design, in keeping with the clean lines and rustic nature of the overall theme.

LEFT: The space under the
stairs is used for storage,
but is left open in order to
increase the sense of light
and space.

BELOW: In a disciplined, pared-down
environment, a few colorful decorative
touches such as these pretty lanterns and
colored glass doorknobs (BOTTOM) add
that special sparkle.

ABOVE: The colors and textures of nature appeal to all: bread and croissants (LEFT) and cut wood (CENTER and RIGHT) sit in simple containers against a very plain background.

NATURAL SHADES

Washable loose covers in white are a practical, yet stylish, way of covering armchairs, which may be placed around a log fire. Anyone who has ever been to New England is aware of the importance of log fires and log stoves. With the abundance of trees, and frigid winter temperatures, the log fire or stove is the symbol of winter warmth and protection.

Simple pottery or china in neutral or natural shades, or white, fits best with this look, and there are no pictures or ornaments. In the early colonial days, fine china and porcelain – if people could afford it – was supplied and imported by English factories, Later the colonists produced their own thick cream or white-colored china, often known as creamware or stoneware. Huge stoneware jars were found in every household to store pickled vegetables, home-made beer, oils – in fact anything that needed to be kept over the winter. Chunky white or cream plates and mugs are an intrinsic part of American style; the influence of the early settlers can still be detected in the thick mugs and plates that are used in American diners and cafés today.

These items – bare wood, white or neutral china, log fires, and lack of ornamentation – create a very contemporary look, but it's worth stopping to reflect that it was a style created by hardship, and of learning how to make the best of limited resources in a challenging climate. The patina of objects is an important element in this style: look for items that are worn, handmade, or show the natural grain of wood or stone. Never restore anything more than you need to in order to make it safe to use – traces of old paint or a faded fabric confirm authenticity.

URBAN COUNTRY

RIGHT: These storage jars
have a sleek ceramic finish
which is combined
with a traditional shape.
Displaying them on
an open shelf is very
much the classic country
kitchen style.

LEFT: The juxtaposition of the natural and
the purely man-made is shown here.
Formica counter tops with wooden
edging and steel uprights create a
contemporary and practical look.

THIS IS THE MOST CONTEMPORARY of the country kitchens, and shows how you can adapt a few key elements of a country look in an otherwise purely modern décor. This large, light kitchen is in a basement of a town house, and the owner, stylist Liz Bauwens, wanted a friendly country kitchen with a contemporary feel. A relaxing atmosphere and room for children to run in and out from the garden were her main criteria. City kitchens today can be similar in style to steel operating theatres – slick and smart – but country kitchens become too often associated with clutter. This kitchen takes three elements from a country kitchen – an Aga cooking range, the use of real wood for some of the furniture and trims, and the idea of creating open space – and makes them work organically with the architecture of the house.

Many of the design principles – a few cabinets, a mix of china and glass, and many displayed items – evoke a country kitchen, but how they are put together is very modern.

LEFT: Here contemporary design has been combined with traditional materials: wooden chairs by designer Arne Jacobsen and a marine ply table with a Formica "surfboard" top which is supported by steel legs.

RIGHT: The white Aga kitchen range is the focal point of the room. The alcoves on either side have been left empty to create an airy feel. The wall by the window is false, and conceals steel security grilles which can be drawn shut over the French windows for protection when the house is empty.

THE STARTING POINT

THE AGA, A SYMBOL OF TRADITION, was the starting point. Yet, because it is white, in a white room, it looks completely modern – clean and stylish. This enormous cooking range makes a big focal statement in the room, so Liz Bauwens decided to leave its surroundings as airy as possible. In the alcoves on either side of the chimney, there is a low table and chest, instead of the ceiling-length cabinets that might otherwise have been installed. This allows the architecture of the room to be on display. The high shelf for pans, and a long rail for hanging kitchen implements, have been fitted discreetly, without altering the proportions of the room. If you have any interesting features in your room, perhaps a chimney, a big window, an alcove, or just an oddly shaped room, you give the scheme more warmth and character if you show them off, rather than covering them up with standard cabinets.

Because of the generous width of the room, a central island, designed by furniture maker David Coote, was a good option. The debate over whether or not to have a central island is important in the design of any kitchen. An island adds a friendly

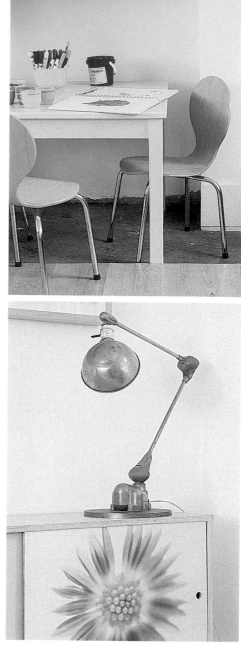

LEFT: If you take a theme
for china, such as white,
blue-and-white, or floral,
you can mix the patterns
and styles together
without creating a
cluttered, untidy look.

LEFT: In the living part of the kitchen, a miniature table and chairs (ABOVE) has been included for the children. A new take on flowers – this big floral design has been painted in a stylized fashion on the front of one of the cabinets (BELOW).

RIGHT: White china and clear glass are displayed on open shelves for a clean, streamlined appearance. The ingredients of this kitchen design, such as natural wood and a marble counter top for food preparation, are timeless, but the clean styling of this chest of drawers (FAR RIGHT) makes it entirely contemporary.

RIGHT: Use a central island to divide the kitchen into specific work areas: the dishwasher faces china and glass storage cabinets and a double sink unit is conveniently close to the stove and oven. An inexpensive chest with simple pull-out drawers (FAR RIGHT) has been included to hold small items. It can also be painted to suit different color schemes.

OPPOSITE: Some shapes, such as the jug of wooden spoons (LEFT), and the coffee pot (RIGHT), are more traditional in style, but others, such as the faucet (CENTER), are strictly modern, yet they all work well together.

BELOW: Make the most of a room's natural architecture by using free-standing chests or tables rather than full-length cabinets, as this keeps the atmosphere as airy and light as possible. Here, pots, cooking implements and ingredients – along with contemporary photography – are all on display, almost farmhouse style.

work area that faces the room, and offers a good way to break up a large space. However, an island does not use space efficiently in a smaller room. Unlike a central table, it cannot be moved and so is relatively inflexible. This central island features a sink, waste-disposal unit, and a beech work surface for food preparation, which makes the journey from the cooker to the sink short and easy. It is also means that, with small children around, it is safer, because food preparation and cooking are then limited to one small area in a large room – another good trick for making living in a large kitchen less demanding.

CLEVER PLANNING

A CENTRAL ISLAND can help kitchen planning enormously by placing working areas close to each other. Here the dishwasher opens facing the other side of the kitchen where the kitchen storage units are located. So when the dishwasher is used, the cutlery, glass, and china can be unloaded directly into the storage cabinets – another labor-saving trick for a large kitchen.

Once again, the white surface is modern, but it has a natural wooden edging to soften the look. Some china and glass kitchenware is kept behind closed doors, while some is out on display. This is another way of making a modern kitchen look relaxed and appear more welcoming.

Having organized the work areas of the kitchen, the eating and play areas were next. Like farmhouse kitchens, kitchens in town houses or city apartments serve as

busy family rooms. They are often the room where everyone gathers not only to eat but also to discuss and plan the day, and where young children might play while their parents cook. One important point to bear in mind when planning a kitchen is to keep the living and playing areas safely away from the oven. Confining certain activities to one area also makes the room easier to tidy: children's books and toys can be stored near where they are needed, for example.

A MODERN AND CLASSIC COMBINATION

A KITCHEN WITH BOTH modern and traditional design elements can have any kind of a kitchen table. A classic pine kitchen table can accentuate the traditional theme, whereas this table's design, based on a surfboard with its slightly rounded edges, emphasizes the contemporary look, as do the chairs from the well-known modernist designer Arne Jacobsen. To keep the look uncluttered, all the storage jars and china are either white, steel, or glass. But there is a friendly assortment of different styles and makes, as if they had all been collected organically over the years rather than having been bought together in one coordinated shopping trip.

Concealing the less attractive aspects of today's world, such as crime prevention measures, also makes the kitchen seem timeless. Here, the French windows at the rear needed security grilles to keep intruders out. To conceal these when they are open, Liz Bauwens had a false "paneled" wall built in front of them, which was painted white like the rest of the room. When they are closed, they just slide between the real wall and the fake paneling, and are completely hidden.

ABOVE: The paneling behind this bowl is false, cleverly concealing the less appealing, but necessary, security grilles.

LIGHT *and* SPACE

The key qualities that distinguish towns from the country are light and space. Instead of being bound by buildings and roads, country dwellers experience the open skies and rambling hills and fields. These pages show how to create a feeling of space and light, even in homes found far from the countryside.

MODERN PASTELS

PASTELS TAKE THEIR INSPIRATION from spring flowers – daffodil yellows, light young greens, lilac, crocus, and hyacinth blues or pale blossom pinks. They are the softest tones in the color spectrum because they have a touch of white in them, turning bright reds, strong blues, and greens chalky or milky. They're often considered "safe" colors because people may feel nervous about using something brighter. But pastels can have a very distinct character of their own, and can create some of the most dramatic, yet easy-to-live with, effects in decorating.

Modern pastels are ideal for making a spare, minimalist room look softer and more inviting, and they're particularly suited to the light found in the northern hemisphere. In cooler countries like Sweden, for example, pastels are traditional decorating shades, while in the hotter Mediterranean countries, much brighter colors are normally used.

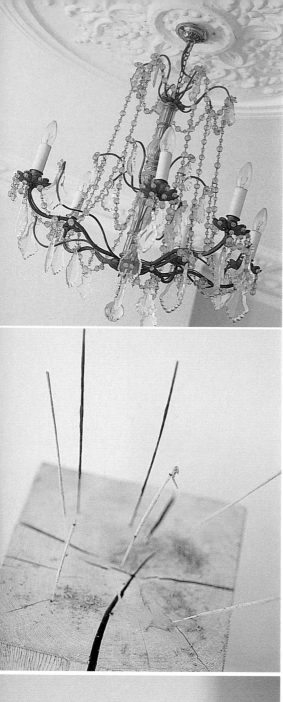

LEFT: Details are important in creating the right atmosphere in a pastel scheme. Mix old and new; the chandelier is an antique, the incense block (CENTER) is a recent design by Janie Jackson, and the doorknob (BOTTOM) is also a modern design.

RIGHT: The impact of pastel colors can be intense if you use a limited number of closely related shades together.

ABOVE: Pastels are literally color with varying amounts of white added – this is why they always look good with white, as is shown here with this painted floor.

OPPOSITE: Adding one outrageous or elaborate touch to a simple scheme adds sparkle.

UNDERSTANDING PASTELS

TONE IS ONE OF THE important clues to understanding pastels. It relates to the depth of color, as pastels of the same tone usually work together well. A pale chalky green sits beautifully with a pale chalky lilac, blue, or tangerine, and they will all mix together to give the effect of fondant icing. If you're using a mix of patterns, such as checks, stripes, and florals, then keeping them in the same tone or depth will make them look as though they belong together.

This doesn't mean that everything in the room needs to be in the same tone, but you should use other tones – such as a vivid splash of purple, or a bright, vibrant red – in small quantities as accent colors. Otherwise, their more strident tones will drown out the delicate murmurings of the pastel shades and overwhelm the scheme.

Pastels team well with white because their shades already contain white. This room has floorboards that have been painted white to reflect the light, and make a room which has only an ordinary amount of natural light seem airy and open. They are also more practical than carpeted white floors, as paint is cheaper to renew than carpet. Having the color – a pale apple green – on the walls when the floor is painted white, also gives a nice twist to the more conventional approach, which is where color is seen on the floor, for example, in a carpet, while the walls remain white.

The furniture is designed by Janie Jackson, and its cool, contemporary lines are softened by the delicate cushion fabrics. Soft pastel silks, with a few stronger colors shot through as a contrast, prevent the look from becoming too austere. Keeping furniture and rooms clean, simple, and bare, while adding ornate touches, such as chandeliers, colored door knobs, and pretty cushions is a light, modern way of using color.

WORKING WITH WHITE

RIGHT: A central pillar in this combined room conceals a bath and shower, but leaves enough space on either side for light to flow through.

LEFT: Contemporary elements – such as modern lamps – look good when mixed with traditional furniture to achieve an effect that is relaxed yet uncluttered. Decorative accessories are either white or the contrast color of green, ensuring a calm atmosphere ideal for a bedroom.

LIGHT AND AIRY, CALM AND FRESH, white is easy to live with and to decorate with. A rustic feeling can be achieved with slightly "soft" white paint, such as limewash, whitewash, and distemper, none of which achieved the bright white we consider normal today. The more brilliant whites have a more modern, urban look – "washing powder" whiteness was not invented until chemical optical brighteners were introduced to paint in the early 1900s.

White makes any space look larger and emphasizes any natural light in the room; and, symbolically, it stands for calm and purity. It is very flexible and "goes" with any and every color.

These qualities make it an ideal choice for rooms where people relax, such as bedrooms, but, to get the best effect, it still requires thought, as the down side of such flexibility is that white rooms can look ordinary.

A good solution is to take a theme, such as white-on-white, white with an accent color used sparingly, or white with one other color in equal partnership. This bedroom is basically white-on-white, with green used as an accent color.

CHOOSING A CONTRAST COLOR

Green is the color of nature, grass, and fields, and represents balance, harmony, and abundance in many cultures, making it a good choice for a room where calm is required, such as a bedroom. This room, unusually, is a combined bedroom-and-bathroom, and color was planned from the first piece that was found for the room – the second-hand double sink. This soft celadon green is married with pure white, and the green is echoed in a delicate leaf pattern on the bedlinen, as well as in the adjacent bathroom with a beautiful Thirties' double sink that was discovered in a second-hand store and re-conditioned.

Flowers and ornaments pick up the theme – it is seen in the grass-green of guelder roses and the innocent green-and-white of lilies-of-the-valley. You could, however, take your color inspiration from a favorite vase, bedspread or bedlinen, a painting, or even the view outside the room. It's a simple but effective way of choosing a color scheme, and one that can be achieved inexpensively.

The objects on the mantelpiece are a romantic mix of family photographs and *objets trouvés*, but there is an underlying theme of glass, metal, and white that makes them all sit together in perfect harmony. The picture frames are made from cheap pine and bought in bulk from a do-it-yourself store chain, then roughly painted with white emulsion to give them a driftwood look. There's a distressed daisy mirror in a weathered frame by Janie Fox, an etched glass candle holder from a local store, an embroidered bedspread from an Indian market, and an old-fashioned dresser, which was found in an antique shop and painted white. The only really extravagant touch is the green shot velvet throw which covers the bed – it is a brilliant statement of color that truly transforms the room.

ABOVE AND LEFT: When you work in a limited color spectrum – here it is white and green, with "white" metals such as silver and natural tones or clear glass blending in – you can easily combine traditional and modern vases, jugs, and other accessories.

LEFT AND ABOVE: In this white bedroom, the color element – green – comes from the lavish velvet bedspread and an embroidered Indian throw. The theme or color scheme could easily be transformed quickly and inexpensively by changing the bedding and switching around a few accessories, which is another great advantage of working with white.

ABOVE: Delicate pastel lampshades add sparkle to the scheme. Buy washcloths, towels, soaps, and bath crystals that echo the decorative feel (RIGHT). Subtle pastels, with a hint of gray, are more natural and less synthetic than sugar-candy shades, and partner contemporary materials well, such as weathered or "white" metals (e.g. silver,) and bleached or pale woods.

LEFT: This renovated Thirties' double-sink (FAR LEFT) was found in a junk shop and inspired the color scheme. Bathroom paraphernalia and family photographs sit side by side (TOP). Colored photo frames work well within the scheme (CENTER). The faucets are original (BOTTOM) and have been renovated to work with modern plumbing systems.

Green married with white is sophisticated and has a feeling of fresh air. Here the kind of miscellaneous items you might find at a country auction have been made elegant by painting them all white: old gilt mirrors are now matt white, as are the French-style dressing table and picture frames. If you don't have the money to fully restore old pieces – a lick of white paint quickly revives them and gives a room a calm, contemporary feel.

THE PRACTICALITIES

If you want to replicate a spacious bedroom-bathroom in your own home, be aware of other practicalities beyond the decorating theme. The advantages of combining the two rooms is that you gain light and space, but you will lose some privacy.

However, even more important, you must ensure that water and electricity never mix. Lighting and sockets must be installed well away from any water sources, and all lighting in the bathroom area must be sealed off. Never use standard lamps or electrical appliances anywhere near the bath or sink areas.

Here, this centrally positioned bath has a shower, and the curved wall-cum-screen encircling the bath provides sufficient protection from the shower spray. Other plumbing considerations include providing some kind of slope to let the water drain away. Here, the bath has been built up slightly to allow a change of level for the water to flow away easily.

Don't compromise on fixtures and fittings, and check carefully that plumbing works. A bath in a bedroom is luxurious only when it works well – without plumbing problems.

LIVING WITH WORK

RIGHT: A white theme looks right with white or pale gray filing cabinets, which help to keep the whole space feeling light and spacious.

LEFT: The desk top has been inexpensively made from a straight piece of wood, and open shelving holds stationery, files, and other storage boxes. Built-in drawers on the last shelf house pens, pencils, stamps, and other small stationery items.

WORKING FROM HOME challenges you to make a home office that is efficient and yet looks as good as the rest of the house. If you are spending any real amount of time working at home, then it's worth spending some money and effort to decorate your work space. After all, part of the dream of working from home is to enjoy an office with a more pleasant environment than one in an office building. Your productivity and sense of achievement will always be better in an enjoyable space with well-planned storage. Essentially a busy space, the home office needs to be efficient, but calm and ordered.

This office, designed by Janie Jackson, has plenty of open storage, so that everything is within easy reach. The desk top is a straight piece of wood, into which has been built two filing cabinets and a set of wire drawers. Three rows of shelves run the length of the small room, and one has narrow drawers, with almost endless storage for small stationery items.

ABOVE: Vases and bottles line the window sill (TOP).

RIGHT: A thin "window" cut between the two rooms helps to increase the light in the office area.

ABOVE: Slim drawers under the bottom shelf (LEFT) ensure plenty of storage for small office necessities such as paper clips and pens. Good lighting is critical in home offices (CENTER), so make sure you plan it properly. Accounting books, files, and folders can all be neatly stored on the shelves (RIGHT).

PLANNING REQUIREMENTS

BEFORE BUILDING ANY SHELVING or buying any furniture for the home office, consider the room's electrical and lighting requirements. You'll need a good working light for both day and night use. This office has opaque Perspex shutters designed by Janie Jackson to allow in maximum light while still retaining privacy. This is important for those regularly working at a computer screen, as they cut out reflective glare.

More natural light has been reclaimed by cutting a narrow, high-up "window" between the office and the room behind it, which acts as a temporary showroom for Janie's designs and samples. This means that borrowed light from the sunnier front room helps to make the north-facing back room brighter. An angled desk light is essential, so that you can adjust the light to where it's needed. And it is important to consider how many sockets you'll need for computers, printers, or photocopiers, for example. Here, a gap has been allowed for cables to run behind the back of the desk area, to plug sockets on that wall, so that there is no chance of any electrical wiring spreading across the room and tripping people.

WELL-PLANNED STORAGE

STORAGE IS THE OTHER critical area to think about, and anyone setting up an office at home for the first time generally underestimates the amount of storage any business will require in the first year. Always try to provide more storage than you think you'll need.

You'll need a place for your computer, fax, telephone (or two, to have a dedicated outgoing line), answering machine, filing cabinets, drawers for stationery, and shelves for reference books or magazines. You can buy or build flexible modular shelf, storage, and desk systems, which are easy to modify as your business grows.

Above: A spare room next to the office provides a showroom.

Left: A long strip of white-painted desk offers plenty of work area but does not take up much room. The upright post at the end of the desk offers useful wall space.

Decorating style

The basics of an office – filing cabinets, computers, and printers – are not very decorative, and the enormous volume of paperwork, samples, and general clutter that most businesses generate doesn't help either. Choosing a single color or using a range of tones can create calm in the chaos.

In this office, the scheme is a basic white one with touches of black or dark gray as an accent. This looks sophisticated and helps the room seem lighter, but it is relatively easy and inexpensive. The filing boxes are steel, which reflects light, and others are dark metallic gray. Having lots of boxes and files that look the same streamlines the look. While styles change frequently, these shown here are office classics that will probably always be available. A laptop computer and fax answering machine in severe black fit in well in these surroundings.

As your home office is entirely yours, you can also decide to work surrounded by color, but allow yourself some flexibility. Painting one wall in a vivid color (orange or purple, for example, are both considered the colors of creativity, while turquoise is supposed to stimulate new ideas) is relatively easy to change if you get tired of it. You can also use metal spray paints on filing cabinets and use storage boxes in fashionable shades. Pattern – such as in chintzy sofas or busy wallpapers – is probably the least flexible and professional-looking option, and will also accentuate the natural clutter of work spaces.

111

OLD *and* NEW

COUNTRY TRADITIONS LAST FOR GENERATIONS, AND
PRECIOUS POSSESSIONS ARE PASSED DOWN THROUGH
THE YEARS. THE SENSE OF TIMELESSNESS THEY GIVE CAN
BE COMBINED WITH CONTEMPORARY DESIGN TO MAKE A
HOUSE REALLY FEEL LIKE A HOME.

BAZAAR STYLE

THIS L-SHAPED STUDIO ROOM in a tall, terraced house was decorated by Sam Robinson, who co-owns the cult clothing and interiors shop, The Cross, in London's Notting Hill. An eclectic, bazaar style is one of the most welcoming and vibrant ways of decorating a home. It is easy to think that this is a style that piles clutter on clutter, but, in fact, there are a few underlying themes that pull it all together, although they are never adhered to so slavishly that they intrude on the relaxed atmosphere.

In this room, flashes of red and vivid pink catch the eye. They're warm, welcoming colors, and yet they also make a dramatic impact. These elements – a vibrant pink picture and pillow, scarlet sofa pillows and red flowers – anchor the collections, but they are also a small enough part of the scheme to be exchanged for another vivid hues – lime green, perhaps, zingy tangerine, or blues and aquas – when fashions change.

RIGHT: A contemporary approach, with a floral painting showing that flowers don't have to be depicted as frilly or feminine.

LEFT: Every home has a few inherited pieces – use them to add age and character to a scheme. Here, an old linen press has been filled with clothes. Vases and pillows have been collected over time.

THE PALETTE

THE FIRST STEPS HERE WERE SIMPLE to achieve. The walls were painted white with a hint of pink in it to warm it up, offering the maximum flexibility to change colors and decorative schemes whenever necessary.

The floorboards had been painted like a checkerboard by a previous owner. They had become very worn, but their slightly peeling effect was part of their charm so they were not altered. Shabby chic is an established style and one that works very well in an eclectic decorative mix, so always think carefully before renovating a piece of furniture. If the furniture has any value, renovation may actually reduce it. For example, restoring old silvered mirrors that have gone cloudy makes them worth less.

Sofas are also part of the background palette, because they are expensive to change. However, this can be overcome by using colorful blankets as throws.

RIGHT: There are literally no rules to this eclectic style: vases, pillows, and ornaments, such as this Hawaiian doll (BOTTOM LEFT), sit side-by-side in a riot of color.

RIGHT: The mantelpiece over the fireplace is crowded with pictures and other items, both old and new, that sit happily together.

LEFT: Mix different objects that have been bought, found, and made. Here are jugs and vases with inset mirrors (TOP LEFT), a Victorian glass pendant twined into a wall lamp (TOP RIGHT), a vintage light (BOTTOM LEFT), and seashells that are glued around a door handle (BOTTOM RIGHT).

A MIX OF CULTURES

EVERY SURFACE HERE IS crowded with bits and pieces from all over the world – from Chinatown in London and New York, from flea markets, fashionable boutiques, and antique shops. They include a mix of old and new, cheap and expensive, handmade pieces, and mass-produced items. There are no set rules, but the advice from Sam Robinson is to be as bold as possible. Her magpie eye picks things up in markets all over the world, and she is never afraid to put a stone Buddha next to a plastic cowboy, or a faded flag next to a modern painting.

"Crowding" is a well known decorative technique, where the sum is more effective than any individual part. "Crowding" means that one or two valuable or intrinsically beautiful items are juxtaposed with less striking, but nevertheless interesting, pieces to create a vibrant, welcoming scheme. There's no responsibility for any particular

ABOVE: The wardrobe was bought from an antique shop (RIGHT), then the doors were removed so that the clothes inside could become part of the decoration. The chest of drawers was found in a flea market.

LEFT: Use small amounts of opulent fabrics, such as tiny silk cushions, large old mirrors, and real candlelight to create a Bohemian and exotic look.

piece to be valuable or perfect, and nothing is taken too seriously – often something that would look completely inappropriate when displayed on its own can be enchanting within a group. It's enough for something to be pretty, to provide a brilliant flash of color, to make people laugh, to remind you of a happy time, or just simply to be. This approach does away with a conventional notion of what is "good taste" and replaces it with fun, *joie de vivre,* and a sense of timelessness.

FLORAL PATTERN

ALTHOUGH THERE ARE MANY different patterns in this room, flowers are a repeated element. They appear painted on a screen, embroidered on a throw, printed on pillows, and painted on jugs and vases. There are real blooms and silk ones, little floral details, and big floral statements.

Mirrors are positioned on almost every wall to reflect light, and the huge, floor-to-ceiling windows have only a thin piece of voile fabric covering them. The curtain is simply hemmed and hung, so that, if a change of style is needed, it will be cheap and easy to achieve. Making a larger investment in curtains can commit you to a specific style for longer than you may want.

LEFT: The eclectic look works just as well in kitchens, where it can distract the eye from outdated fittings such as this white Seventies' faucet and sink.

ABOVE: Anything beautiful – or anything that you love – can be part of a decorative scheme. These slippers and bag are too colorful to hide away (CENTER). Before completely changing a serviceable kitchen, see if altering one or two key details will update it. This kitchen is equipped with Fifties' finds, such as floral storage jars (LEFT). Such things are not genuine antiques and are still very reasonably priced in flea markets, garage, or tag sales.

STORAGE AND DECORATION

IN ANY STUDIO APARTMENT, storage is always a problem and here, items of clothing, purses, and shoes are all displayed on open shelves. They hang from rails or are even arranged on table tops as part of the decorative detail.

The wardrobe door has been removed to reveal the clothes inside, almost as if they are on display for sale in a market bazaar. When you have pretty things, such as embroidered bags or shoes, it seems a pity not to enjoy them all the time rather than just when they're worn. However, there is a limit to what you want to see, and one good trick employed here is to put winter or summer clothes in storage to free up space.

At one end of the L-shape is a kitchen which contains mass-market cabinets. By changing the wall tiling and the cabinets' handles, and painting them white to match the rest of the room, the fact that the style was not the owner's choice was made less important. The bathroom, too, was not renewed, but, to liven it up, thousands of pretty shells have been stuck in a border on the walls and as a feature around the door handle.

To glue shells, or other decorative items, to a wall, you'll need a good household glue, such as polyvinyl adhesive or epoxy resin, both of which are available from home improvement stores.

If you're going to glue shells to something that's going to be used regularly, such as a door handle, make sure that they don't stick out so much that you'll graze your hand every time your turn the knob. Alternatively, you could adopt a more cautious version of the look by just gluing some shells to picture frames or mirror surrounds, rather than fixing them to walls or doors.

ETHNIC

RIGHT: This look has no matching items, and things are not bought to go with each other or in sets, which makes for a very relaxed air of abundance in a room.

LEFT: Rich colors, such as dark green, deep royal blue, or this warm, opulent red make good backgrounds for the ethnic look, and make the room seem both cosy and grand, and provide a superb background for displaying a range of pictures.

MODERN COUNTRY INTERIORS, with their pared-down and airy look, contrast sharply with decorating influences from the Far East, Middle East and Africa. Artifacts from travels abroad can add vibrant touches to rooms that are otherwise classically American – an original and attractive blending of East and West.

From the East and the Middle East come ocher, cinnabar red, black, and vermilion, with fretwork carvings, intricate patterns, and rich dark woods. Brilliant silks come from India, while regal colors and patterns emerge from the old Moorish empire and are still found in Morocco today. Individual items need not be costly – many collectibles are affordable both here and in their own country. Look for rich colors and ornate patterns, and don't be afraid to mix styles and cultures.

ABOVE: A colorful tribal hat with exotic decoration that was bought on an Eastern trip is proudly displayed in this room.

LEFT: This mantelpiece has not been "arranged" although larger items are on the outer ends, and smaller pieces in the middle, mixing eastern and western pottery and china. In this look, the whole is more than the sum of the parts – just keep adding and taking away pieces until you like the look of it, but change it around from time to time to enjoy new pieces.

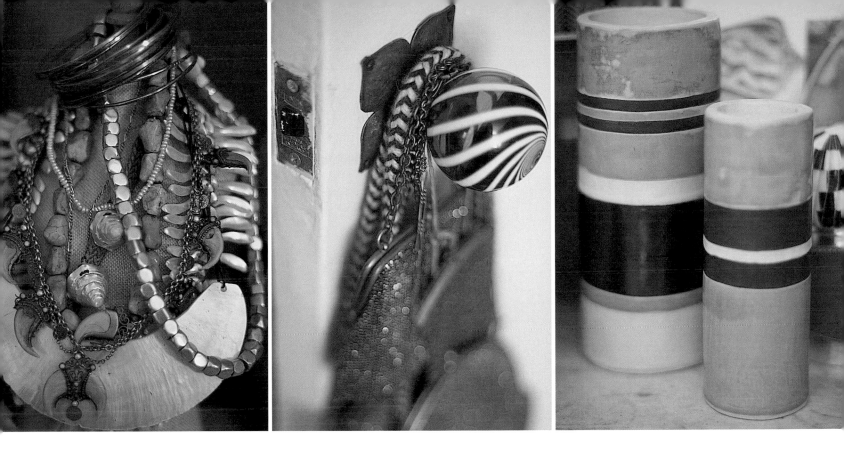

AN INSPIRED STYLE

THE ETHNIC LOOK HAS EVOLVED as a rich, global-inspired style, mixing Indian silks with Persian carpets, Moroccan glasses, tribal rugs, and African artifacts in one glorious symphony. Once again, there are no rules, but, while the New England look relies on discipline and restraint, the ethnic style is all about opulence. This is the sitting room of Lucinda Chambers, who chose a white background for her rose-inspired kitchen. Here, however, she knew she wanted a strong rich color. After considering a deep green, she settled on this rich red, a perfect background for pictures, and a color that is both grand and cozy. She painted large strips of several colors and took several months to decide on exactly the right shade. While the cool, pared-down interiors of some cultures look best with pale woods, such as pine, beech, elm, and unstained oak, this is a look in which to use the luxurious patina of the darker or mid-tone woods, such as cherrywood and mahogany.

Here, a combination of East and West is found: kilim cushions are beside velvet embroidered ones; African tribal art is placed adjacent to a contemporary sketch, and American-made lamps rest on an intricate Moroccan mosaic table. While cities all over the world have evolved as one, with the same international brands on sale and many of the fashions following each other, it is in the countryside that great artwork, craftsmanship and design survive, so this ethnic look will keep alive traditions that may otherwise be lost. Lucinda changes things around constantly – she believes that a house is never "done," or finished; and that if you enjoy finding things, then it's always worth altering and refining the balance in a room to display them in interesting ways.

ABOVE: Twine jewelry around door handles or a bust (LEFT AND CENTER) instead of locking it away in a jewelbox. An air of age and wear adds character, as seen in these containers (ABOVE).

127

LEFT: Reds, pinks, and browns dominate the collections found in this room: this Eastern vase is delicately etched, yet sits well with bolder pieces. Beadwork (CENTER) is another theme, to be found on items displayed around the room, and also on pillows. Don't be afraid of clashing colors – the pink of this rose is wonderful against the red walls. In this look, more is more – be as extreme and daring as you want to be. Paint and accessories can easily be changed if you change your mind.

RIGHT: Photo frames, each one different from the next, hold family photos. Flowers (FAR RIGHT) echo the warm pinks and reds of the room. Instead of a plain lampshade, choose an exotic swirling design to echo the rest of the room (BOTTOM RIGHT). Collections of embroidery and mosaics, including this pair of boots (BOTTOM LEFT), are on display rather than being hidden away.

HOW TO BUY ABROAD

EVERYONE IS FAMILIAR WITH souvenir syndrome. You go abroad, see wonderful things in the shops and markets, but when you bring them home they often look out of place. Yet many people who travel frequently often have beautiful homes, crammed full of things which act as pleasing mementoes. As one of the world's top fashion directors, Lucinda travels constantly, and her home is filled with beautiful items she has found in flea markets and shops everywhere. The old adage "buy only what you love" – invaluable advice when buying art or antiques – stands good for buying ethnic goods abroad. If you buy to fill a gap, for example, says Lucinda, then that's when you make mistakes.

It's also important to find out a bit about what the area is best known for – rugs in Turkey and Morocco, for example, or silks in India, and ask local people, either friends or hotel staff, where the best sources are. Find time to visit without buying – simply walking round and looking at everything, and assessing prices will give you an idea of what you can get for your budget. It's a mistake to equate "ethnic" with cheap, or to buy something because you thought you saw it back home at three times the price. Those will have been bought by a professional buyer familiar with current tastes, who makes sure that the quality is good. You may well be looking at a cheap version in the country of origin. Once you've established what a fair price is, and roughly judged a good piece, because you've seen several examples, you're better informed to buy.

Of course, the trade that was established by the Silk Routes and the Spice Trails centuries ago still goes on today, and you can buy ethnic artifacts in every major world city, so buying when you return home is an option, particularly if want antiques or second-hand items. A rug, for example, could have been made in the Middle East in the 19th century, spent 100 years on a floor in Britain, and be available for sale in the United States. Once again, buy because you love the shape and color, or find out as much as you can about the category – whether it be Delft porcelain, Venetian mirrors, or Chinese lacquerwork – before buying for yourself.

Great ESCAPES

EVERYONE NEEDS TIME OUT AND A
PLACE TO GO WHERE THE NOISY
WORLD CANNOT FOLLOW. A GARDEN
RETREAT, HOWEVER TINY, A LOFT
ROOM TUCKED AWAY IN THE EAVES OF
THE HOUSE, A COUNTRY COTTAGE,
EVEN A VINTAGE AIRSTREAM, ALL OFFER
THE POTENTIAL TO CREATE A
FANTASY INTERIOR — A CLOSED
DOOR BETWEEN YOU
AND THE WORLD.

OUTDOOR RETREAT

RIGHT: The retreat, filled with wicker furniture, is built along the end of a long and narrow town garden. You can easily build a summerhouse that looks as if it has been there for generations.

LEFT: Soft candlelight, a hammock and luminous cushions in Indian silk make this veranda seem part of somewhere wild and distant, rather than the middle of a city. Don't be afraid of taking accessories outside – there's no need to stick to "normal" garden furniture.

THIS RETREAT IS MORE than just a shed at the end of a long, narrow town backyard. It's an echo of the architecture from the childhood of its designer, Hazel Collins. She took the design from the verandas of Savannah, Georgia, and added on a room for peace and meditation. In the middle of city life, her aim was to feel close to nature, and also to have a special space to get away from the constant noise and bustle.

The retreat runs across the end of the backyard, and two-thirds of the building is a covered veranda, with the other third a small square room that is painted white. Constructed in wood that has been tongue and grooved by joiners, it has stout hanging hooks to hold a big comfortable hammock. Wicker furniture painted in happy jewel shades of blue and lilac adds to the relaxed, calm atmosphere of this special place.

RIGHT AND BELOW: The "veranda" runs across two-thirds of the backyard and is deep enough to take a dinner table and chairs for romantic dining by candlelight on summer nights. The remaining third is the adjoining "meditation" room, painted white, which takes up the rest of the space across the backyard.

SHADY SPACE

FOR ALL ITS FEELINGS of light and sunshine, the retreat is located at the northern end of a south-facing backyard, and is also heavily overshadowed by big trees. So the little room has been painted white inside to maximize the light, and all the furniture and curtains are in bright, pastel shades, as if to echo reflected sunlight. There are Indian silks, fitting for the colonial atmosphere, which are light enough to add reflection and sparkle.

The paint on the outside of the retreat takes its hue from nature. The blue color reflects the pale light of the northern skies, and fits beautifully with the natural vegetation of the abundant and much-loved backyard around it. Paint can seem intrusive in the backyard, but, generally speaking, the subtler the color, and the closer to nature that it appears, the more likely it is to blend with the surrounding flowers and shrubs.

The light in the northern hemisphere, even on a sunny day, is predominantly blue, so it is the cooler blues and purples that work best in such backyards. If you want to create an outside retreat nearer to the equator, you can use brighter colors and white, (these can look a little bleak under northern skies.) Under a soft, gray sky, subtle blues and purples will look rich; oranges and warm yellows will look warm under almost any sky; and earth tones will work anywhere. Bright colors can be brought in as spot accents, such as in pillows, that can be taken outside on a sunny day and hastily retrieved when the sky clouds over. As you move further south – to California, Texas, or the Mexican border – vivid colors become more appropriate.

ABOVE: Wicker furniture is inexpensive, and can be painted or dressed up in silk and velvet. There is a very contemporary mix of ancient and modern, and of East and West on the veranda: the china accessories and wicker furniture are Victorian, but the cool, uncluttered way they are presented is very modern. The luxurious cushions are made from Indian silk.

RIGHT: Graceful lilies and the glow of several candles add to the atmosphere for evening dining. Use lots of candles, but protect them by using glass shades, or dropping nightlights into glasses or glass jars (but never leave them unattended.)

FOLK
MEMORIES

RIGHT: It's the detail that makes the difference. The timeless designs, simply hand-painted in bright colors, and folkloric styles on this gypsy caravan can still be found today on painted tinware, toleware and handcrafted wooden items sold at craft fairs or in country shops. Link them with equally simple, classic prints to create the feel of an old country home.

LEFT: Traditional folk patterns and bright innocent colors, such as reds and yellows, are the starting point for a cottage-style scheme that can be adapted from this Victorian gypsy caravan to transform the plainest bedrooms into a sanctuary reminiscent of fields and flowers. Floral prints plus one or two relatively humble antiques or collectibles can turn the tiniest space into a special and personal place.

THERE'S A CERTAIN KIND of cottage style, based on floral cotton prints, humble wild flowers, and simple materials such as cotton, tin, and wood that travelled with the earliest settlers and can still be found today. It's a perfect decorating look for an escapist – whether for a bedroom in the eaves, a clapboard house in the woods, or, as shown here, in a restored antique wagon that originally belonged to European gypsies. Yet it has enough character of its own to make a modern box bedroom look like a cottage in the fields.

The charm of these patterns lies in their innocence and timelessness – there is nothing grand or over-stated. Floral cotton prints take their inspiration from gardens and fields, colors are light and bright, and everything is pretty and relaxed. It's a perfect backdrop for collectibles, and, because nothing matches, a great way of using up scraps of material bought cheaply in sales or left over from larger projects.

ABOVE AND LEFT: To
achieve a relaxed,
cottage-like look, don't
match patterns. Here each
pillow is different. Using a
whole range of reds –
from bright pinks to
scarlet, poppy, and berry
reds – is a successful way
of working with one color.
Yellow, red, and white are
the only three colors used.
Limiting the number of
colors looks very
contemporary.

RIGHT: Use floral fabrics which have lots
of white in their backgrounds to help
keep an atmosphere light and airy. Add
extra touches like the bobble trim on the
voile, and bring in a few scraps of antique
fabric, such as the old blue French quilt.

Even the sewing techniques won't challenge novice needleworkers. The casual way that scraps are sewn together to make light, informal curtains is the key. Cushions are in lots of different fabrics, and have few trimmings. Curtains are hung straight, on simple ties or hooks, and there are no elaborate pelmets or tie-backs to make the room feel cluttered.

It is color and pattern, of the most vibrant, upbeat kind, that really defines this look. There are literally dozens of different floral patterns, many of them classics that are still made today, in a tiny space, to create a welcoming and happy scheme. The way these are put together shows that almost anything goes – vivid modern magenta pinks are side-by-side with deep Victorian maroon, and delicate florals with checks and stripes. Light butter muslins and friendly, traditional wool blankets are contrasted textures.

How to mix patterns

THERE ARE NO RULES TO THIS COTTAGE LOOK, but there are some helpful tips. The first is to create unity of color. Choose two, or at the most three, main colors and use them to link diverse patterns and forms. Here the overall theme is yellow and red – ranging from palest cream to hot magenta pinks. There's also a hint of blue in the antique chair and the rug on the bed. In a small space – and many sanctuaries are very small – this color unity should extend to the walls and even woodwork. Here the walls are a buttery yellow and the outside of the caravan a deep red. In a room inside try using the stronger color, red, as an unexpected trim for woodwork, window frames or even as a paint color for the floor.

Working across the spectrum of one color

THE USE OF COLOR IN THIS CARAVAN also illustrates the way you can work right across the spectrum of one color. Here a full range of red has been used, from candyfloss pinks, classic red ginghams, berry reds to deep maroon. The same effect could have been

achieved with blues, yellows, or greens. If you put two different reds together – or two different blues or greens – they may clash, but, if you pile on more shades and tones, then the whole look acquires unity, along with depth and vibrancy. This is a trick of contemporary interior decorators to make a color scheme look lively and natural.

Mix old and new

Just one or two interesting collectibles can transform an interior decorated with inexpensive fabrics into an intensely personal space. Here a few Victorian items – an iron lighting sconce, a fireplace with its own inset mirror and a classic wicker chair set the scene. Those traditional objects actually mix well with more recent collectibles, such as brightly colored Fifties' tablecloths, pastel ceramics, or traditional country pottery. Garden antiques, such as old watering cans, porch chairs, potting tables, even sections of wrought iron fencing, garden tools, sap buckets, or flower urns, would suit this floral style well and evoke memories of the great outdoors. Don't overload the room – just a few pretty, aged pieces, such as this camping "Kelly" kettle, are enough to conjure up the country fantasy while keeping the purity and simplicity of the folk look.

ABOVE: There is increasing interest in re-fitting old stoves to houses to re-create a cozy, welcoming feeling. This stove (LEFT) is in full working order, and is used for picnics. Victorian mantelpieces such as this one (RIGHT) can be bought, either as original or reproductions, and make an ideal focus for a traditional room.

AIRSTREAM

RIGHT: A van can be a mobile spare room, a holiday home – here this Airstream is parked on the beach – or it can be placed in a backyard to act as a fantasy hideaway. Stars such as Sean Penn and Tom Hanks have used them as mobile offices or on-location havens.

LEFT: Fifties' Americana is a hot collectible theme now. Here, red curtains and a Stars-and-Stripes bedspread are combined to create a Wild West look.

GREAT ESCAPES DON'T HAVE to be fixed in one place – in fact, to be able to take off, or even, perhaps, just to be able to dream of taking off one day, is sometimes all that you need to create the illusion of escape. This Fifties' Airstream evokes the freedom of the open road, the age of Jack Kerouac, the endless miles of the Arizona desert, and has now become a chic accessory for style addicts and stars. But, when not mobile, and parked at the end of a backyard, it can become an office, special hideaway, or even a spare bedroom for guests. When it is driven away for the holidays, the van can become a portable bedroom for visiting friends.

RETRO STYLE

YET YOU DON'T HAVE TO OWN AN AIRSTREAM to enjoy Fifties' Americana. It is now a hot collecting area – from ceramics and furniture to more unusual items such as flashy

LEFT: In a small living space, one or two distinctive items really add to the atmosphere. This Fifties' lamp was discovered in a second-hand shop. Pillows can help to make the most of your theme: here a wild West design (BELOW) adds a cheerful note to the U-shaped banquettes. These act as seating by day, while at night two mattresses are added to create a huge bed, so that the Airstream can sleep two adults and three children.

RIGHT: This Formica-topped table evokes the Fifties' style. It is a design that is still manufactured today, and it neatly folds up when the banquettes are used as a bed.

vintage eyeglass frames, old store billboards, metal lawn chairs reminiscent of grandma's garden, vintage kitchen items, and colorful printed and patterned textiles from the Forties and Fifties, such as tablecloths. These are still relatively affordable, and a small space, such as a mobile home, is an ideal place to display a complete collection or re-create an entire look. Flea markets and yard sales are always good places to look, as are specialty stores.

You might specialize in a commonly used pattern – such as cherries, roses, checks, or plaids – as well as themes, such as cowboy, Mexicana or items made as tourist souvenirs from vacation spots. The advantage of focussing your buying in this way is two-fold: first, grouping a number of similar items together in the home always looks effective, and second, you will develop a greater knowledge and awareness of particularly sought-after or special items.

Once you have bought an item, it's often best to keep it in its original condition as far as possible, at least until you have discovered enough about it to ascertain whether re-painting or restoring it will affect its value. For everyday items of low intrinsic value, such as lawn chairs, repainting is fine. However, an unrestored and weathered look is what gives the chair the patina of the past.

Be wary, too, of 21st-century cleaning techniques. Putting Fifties' china in a contemporary dishwasher may wear off the pattern in just a few washes, and strong chemicals could destroy vintage fabrics. If you are buying from a specialist dealer, consult them on the correct way to clean collectibles, or look at household cleaning books from the Fifties.

ABOVE: This china, glassware, and plastic was all purchased recently from contemporary home stores, but the cheerful colors and simple shapes, matched with traditional gingham, fit perfectly into the nostalgic theme. Look for simple, classic shapes and bright colors.

OPPOSITE: Vintage kitchen style evokes a nostalgic dream of home-baked apple pie. Some traditional styles of cookware and china are still made today, such as this kettle. Check out the detail – handles and materials are important, as Fifties' kitchens combined "modern" materials such as Formica, with traditional dark woods such as teak. This Fifties' teak chest has a new stove top set into it – an ingenious way of making a kitchen area that looks homey.

You can complete a retro look by purchasing fabrics and items that are still made today. Here the gingham curtains, diner-style plates and Wild West designs on the cushions were found in contemporary home stores, mixing in perfectly with the Stars-and-Stripes bedspread and authentic Fifties' items to create a total theme. Don't choose anything too sophisticated-looking – simple shapes and bright colors will work best. Go for honesty in design – this is not about finding imitations or reproductions, but picking cheerful, innocent patterns and colors that are simply what they've always been.

ABOVE: The Airstream lives in the city but makes frequent visits to the country and the beach.

SMALL SPACE PLANNING

THE AIRSTREAM IS ALSO A LESSON in how to fit a great deal of living space into a small unit, and it's always worth looking at such interiors when planning very small rooms. Here everything is beautifully compact. One end of the Airstream has the double bed, while at the other, a U-shaped banquette of seating around the table has two more mattresses stowed away beneath it. At night the table is folded up, and the banquette opens out into a massive bed for up to three children, or another adult couple. The hob is fitted into the top of a chest of drawers, and most of the lighting is fixed to the walls. On one side, a detachable awning can be pulled out to create a shady place to enjoy drinks at sundown or shield holidaymakers from the heat of the day.

RIGHT: The end of the road. Take designs from the past, put your own contemporary spin on them and turn them into something original and stylish.

150

DIRECTORY

Re-create some of the styles seen in *Country Chic* with the furniture, lighting, bedding, china, and accessories stocked at the outlets whose addresses and contact numbers are listed below. Anyone who loves the looks on these pages will enjoy a visit to any of the shops below whose styles are both contemporary and decorative.

Antiques

Channel Craft
601 Monongahela Ave.
North Charleroi, PA 15022
(724) 489-4900
Vintage Toys

Country Products by Ennis Antiques
R.R. 3, Box 347A
Greentown, PA 18426
(570) 857-0945

Federalist Antiques
515 Park Dr.
Kenilworth, IL 60043
(847) 256-1791

Grunewald Folk Art
P.O. Box 52
Alden, IL 60001
(815) 648-4683

Laura Fisher
1050 Second Ave.
Gallery 84
New York, NY 10002
(212) 836-2596
Antique Quilts and Americana

Maine Street Antiques & Art
110 W. Main St.
West Branch, IA 52358
(319) 643-2065

Mary Jane McCarty
(215) 428-1808
Antique textile pillows

Monroe Saltworks
Stovepipe Alley
P.O. Box 820
Monroe, ME 04951
(207) 525-4471
www.monroesaltworks.com

Village Chairs and Wares
402 Main St.
Port Jefferson, NY 11764
(516) 473-2646
www.shop-portjeff.net

Woodard & Greenstein
American Antiques
506 E. 74th St.
New York, NY 10021
(212) 988-2906

Lighting

Brass Light Gallery
131 S. First St.
Milwaukee, WI 53204
(800) 243-9595

Heritage Lanterns
25 Yarmouth Crossing Dr.
Yarmouth, ME 04096
(207) 846-3911

Lando Lighting
210 Clarence Street
Brampton, ON L6W 6S2
(905) 984-8727

Period Lighting Fixtures
167 River Rd.
Clarksburg, MA 01247
(413) 664-7141
(800) 828-6990

Superlite
1901 Cogan Ave.
Winnipeg, MB R2R 0H6
(204) 989-7277

Floral, Classic and Contemporary Fabrics, Furnishings, and Bedlinen

Atlantic Blanket Co.
Swane Island, ME 04865
(207) 526-4492

Bennison Fabrics
76 Greene St.
New York, NY 10012
(212) 941-1212

Cottage Classics
R.R. 1, Box 85
Loysvilly, PA 17047
(717) 789-9375

Country Curtains
(800) 456-0321
Catalog/mail order

Cuddledown of Maine
(800) 323-6793
Catalog/mail order

Dakotah
1 N. Park Lane
Webster, SD 57274
(800) DAKOTAH
Home furnishings

Donna Fields Interiors
113 S. Orange Dr.
Los Angeles, CA 90036
(323) 932-1749

Elizabeth Eakins Cotton
1 Marshall St.
South Norwalk, CT 06854
(203) 831-9347

Karen Houghton Interiors
41 N. Broadway
Nyack, NY 10906
(914) 358-0133

Lane Upholstery Group
P.O. Box 849
Conover, NC 28613
(704) 328-2271

Loom Company
28 W. 17th St., Suite 701
New York, NY 10011
(212) 366-7214

New England Classic Interiors
465 Congress St.
Portland, ME 04101
(207) 773-6144

Rags
1618 Euclid St.
Santa Monica, CA 90404
(310) 392-5220

Susan Sargent Designs
Rte. 30
Pawlet, VT 05761
(800) 245-4767

Vermont Country Timeless Designs
P.O. Box 187
Readsboro, VT 05350
(800) 831-7020

CHINA, GLASS, AND ACCESSORIES

AMERICAN HIGGLEDY PIGGLEDY
207 E. Park
Fredericksburg, TX 78624
(830) 997-8520

BACKYARD HEIRLOOMS
P.O. Box 1094
Sheffield, MA 01257
(413) 229-5959
www.backyardheirlooms.com

BLACHERE GROUP
41 Madison Ave.
New York, NY 10010
(800) 641-4808
French flatware

THE CHINA CUPBOARD
1507 Wilmot Place
Victoria, BC V8R 5S3

HEIGHTS GLASS & MIRROR
200 Williams St.
Bensenville, IL 60106
(630) 227-3300
www.euroview.com

KLEIN/REID
475 Keap St.
Brooklyn, NY 11211
(718) 388-9331
Porcelain vases

LESLEE JAGO CERAMICS AND DESIGN
P.O. Box 210
Hailey, ID 83333
(208) 788-1607

UNION STREET GLASS
833 S. 19th St.
Richmond, CA 94804
(888) 451-7752

FLOORING, TILING, AND RUGS

ABC CARPET AND HOME
888 Broadway
New York, NY 10003
(212) 473-3000
www.abchome.com

ATELIER CARPETS
(800) 897-2353

COUNTRY FLOORS
15 E. 16th St.
New York, NY 10003
(212) 627-8300
www.countryfloors.com

CROSSVILLE PORCELAIN STONE TILE
346 Sweeney Dr.
Crossville, TN 38555
(931) 484-2110

FORBO INDUSTRIES
P.O. Box 667
Hazleton, PA 18201
(800) 233-0475
Floor coverings

HARRIS-TARKETT
2225 Eddie Williams Rd.
Johnson City, TN 37601
(800) 842-7816
Hardwood floors

FURNITURE

IMPORT SPECIALISTS
82 Wall St.
New York, NY 10005
(800) 334-4044
Rugs and linens

MULBERRY STREET RUGS
15135 Sunset Blvd., #220
Pacific Palisades, CA 90272
(310) 455-3995

P.G. HARDWOOD FLOORING INC.
2424, rue Principale
Saint-Edouard
Quebec G0S 1Y0
(418) 796-2328

AROUND THE BEND
7883 Cleveland Rd.
Wooster, OH 44691
(330) 345-9585
Willow furniture

BROYHILL FURNITURE
1 Broyhill Pk.
Lenoir, NC 28633
(800) 327-6944

HIBBERTS CABINETRY AND FURNITURE SHOP
7 Townsley Dr.
Cartersville, GA 30120
(770) 382-5863

MAINE COTTAGE FURNITURE
P.O. Box 935
Yarmouth, ME 04096
(207) 846-1430

NEW JERSEY BARN COMPANY
P.O. Box 702
Princeton, NJ 08542
(609) 924-8480

POTLUCK STUDIOS
23 Main St.
Accord, NY 12404
(914) 626-2300

SCHROEDERS FINE FURNITURE
15 N.E. Street
Lebanon, OH 45036
(513) 932-0474

SHAKER WORKSHOPS
P.O. Box 8001
Ashburnham, MA 01430
(800) 840-9121
www.shakerworkshops.com

WHISPERING PINES
(800) 836-4662
Catalog/mail order

GENERAL STORES FOR FURNITURE, LIGHTING, BEDDING, AND ACCESSORIES

AREA
180 Varick St.
New York, NY 10014
(212) 924-7084

BANANA REPUBLIC HOME
(888) 277-8953

L.L. BEAN
(800) 652-4288
Catalog/mail order

CABIN CREEK FARM
P.O. Box 208
Summersville, KY 42782
(270) 932-6277

CALVIN KLEIN HOME
205 W. 39th St.
New York, NY 10018
(212) 719-2600

CARLETON V
979 Third Ave.
New York, NY 10019
(212) 355-4525

CUSTOM DESIGN SHUTTERS
P.O. Box 570
Cibolo, TX 78108
(210) 659-2436
(800) 874-5787

FIELDCREST
1 Lake Circle Dr.
Kannapolis, NC 28081
(800) 841-3336

MEDITERRANEAN LIVING
20 Don Bosco Pl.
Port Chester, NY 10573
(914) 935-9630

NATE'S NANTUCKET BASKETSHOP
171 Eastman Hill Rd.
Sanbornton, NH 03269
(603) 286-8927

PEACOCK ALLEY
1825 Market Center Blvd., Suite 440
Dallas, TX 75207
(800) 810-0708

PIERRE DEUX
870 Madison Ave.
New York, NY 10021
(212) 570-9343
www.pierredeux.net

RALPH LAUREN HOME COLLECTION
867 Madison Ave.
New York, NY 10021
(212) 606-2100

C.J. SPRONG & COMPANY
300 Pleasant St.
Northampton, MA 01060
(413) 584-7440

THREE GIRLS
4430 Broadway
Boulder, CO 80304
(303) 413-1303

VINTAGE BASKETS
20212 87th Ave. South
Kent, WA 98031
(253) 395-3131

ACKNOWLEDGMENTS

To my parents and Lois, Milo and Finn

To David, Frederick and Rosalind

Thank you to:

Cath Kidston, Laura Ashley, Sanderson, The Cross, The Shaker
Shop, Graham & Greene, The White Company, Bombay Duck,
Toast, Emma Bernhard, Thomas Goode, Couverture, Jerry's Home
Store, Osborne & Little, Designers Guild, Parma Lilac, Monsoon
Home and The Rug Company.

We'd like to thank the friends who have generously allowed us to
photograph their homes and benefit from their inspiration. Many of
the ideas in this book are the result of their creativity.

INDEX